W9-BTM-374

DECEMBER 1998

Sunday	Monday	Tuesday	Wednesday	Thursday	Friday	Saturday
		1	2	3	4	5
6	7	8	9	10	11	12
13	14	15	16	17	18	19
20	21	22	23	24 Christmas Eve	25 Christmas Day	26
27	28	29	30	31 New Year's Eve		

Christmas
with Southern Living
1998

Oxmoor House

©1998 by Oxmoor House, Inc.
Book Division of Southern Progress Corporation
P.O. Box 2463, Birmingham, Alabama 35201

Southern Living® is a federally registered trademark belonging to
Southern Living, Inc.

All rights reserved. No part of this book may be reproduced in any
form or by any means without the prior written permission of the
publisher, excepting brief quotations in connection with reviews
written specifically for inclusion in magazines or newspapers, or
single copies for strictly personal use.

ISBN: 0-8487-1800-3
ISSN: 0747-7791
Manufactured in the United States of America
First Printing 1998

Editor-in-Chief: *Nancy Fitzpatrick Wyatt*
Senior Homes Editor: *Mary Kay Culpepper*
Senior Foods Editor: *Susan Payne Stabler*
Senior Editor, Editorial Services: *Olivia Kindig Wells*
Art Director: *James Boone*

Christmas with Southern Living 1998

Editor: *Rebecca Brennan*
Food Editor: *Julie Fisher*
Assistant Editor: *Adrienne S. Davis*
Editorial Assistant: *Cecile Y. Nierodzinski*
Copy Editors: *Keri Bradford Anderson, Anne Dickson*
Contributing Editors: *Shannon Sexton Jernigan, Susan Hernandez Ray*
Writer: *Mindy Wilson*
Associate Art Director: *Cynthia R. Cooper*
Designer: *Emily Albright Parrish*
Senior Photographers: *Jim Bathie, John O'Hagan*
Photographer: *Brit Huckabay*
Senior Photo Stylist: *Kay E. Clarke*
Photo Stylists: *Virginia R. Cravens, Linda Baltzell Wright*
Director, Test Kitchens: *Kathleen Royal Phillips*
Assistant Director, Test Kitchens: *Gayle Hays Sadler*
Test Kitchens Staff: *Susan Hall Bellows, Julie Christopher, Michele
    Brown Fuller, Natalie E. King, Elizabeth Tyler Luckett, Andrea
    Noble, Iris Crawley O'Brien, Jan A. Smith*
Illustrator: *Kelly Davis*
Publishing Systems Administrator: *Rick Tucker*
Production and Distribution Director: *Phillip Lee*
Associate Production Manager: *Theresa L. Beste*
Production Assistant: *Faye Porter Bonner*

We're Here for You!

We at Oxmoor House are dedicated to serving you with reliable
information that expands your imagination and enriches your life.
We welcome your comments and suggestions. Please write to us at:

Oxmoor House, Inc.
Editor, *Christmas with Southern Living*
2100 Lakeshore Drive
Birmingham, AL 35209

To order additional publications, call 1-205-877-6560.

CONTENTS

Front cover, clockwise from top: Orange-Date-Nut Cookies (page
120), Mixed Nut Turtles (page 125), Chocolate-Caramel
Thumbprints (page 124), Peppermint Candy Shortbread (page 129),
Coffee Bean Cookies (page 114)

Christmas
with Southern Living®
1998

Edited by Rebecca Brennan,
Julie Fisher, and Adrienne S. Davis

Holiday Home   6

Back cover, top left: Red Berry Wreath, page 10
bottom left: Velvet Pillow, page 22
right: Tablecloth Tree Skirt, page 26

All the Trimmings   42

Suppers to Soirees   62

Gifts of Good Taste   94

HOLIDAY HOME

Red Berry
Wreath

Flower
Wreath

Gardener's
Wreath

Pomegranate
Wreath

GREETINGS FROM EVERY SEASON

These easy-to-assemble wreaths say welcome with the lush reds and greens of the season—and some surprising combinations of flowers, greenery, and edibles. One will suit your holiday style.

RED BERRY WREATH

Create a little drama by foregoing the greenery and letting this simple wreath of stemmed red berries echo both the stark beauty of the wintry season and the warmth inside your home.

To make the wreath, cover a straw wreath with sheet moss, securing the moss with florist's wire. Using florist's wire, bind together approximately 3 stems of holly berries to form a bundle. (For the wreath shown we used 9 bundles.)

Wire the bundles in place around the wreath, overlapping bundles so they all face the same direction.

Use florist's wire to attach the bow. For bow-making directions, see page 145.

To make the garland, wind ribbon around a purchased evergreen garland. Tuck stems of berries among the branches. To make the wreath and garland last from year to year, use artificial berry stems and garland.

POMEGRANATE WREATH

Halved pomegranates accent the traditional holly wreath, reminding guests of one of the joys of the season—luscious things to eat.

To make the wreath, soak clippings of holly overnight in a large container of water. The amount of holly you need will depend on the size of your wreath, which you will need to cover completely.

Thoroughly soak a florist's foam wreath in water. Push the holly stems into the foam, covering the wreath form entirely.

To add the pomegranates, make a cut in the pomegranate, then tear it apart for a natural look. Using a long florist's pick, place 1 end of the pick in the pomegranate half and the opposite end in the wreath base, securing the pomegranate to the wreath. Refer to the photograph for placement ideas. Use florist's wire to attach the bow. For bow-making directions, see page 145.

For a special party or open house, place stems of fresh flowers in water vials, and position the vials in the wreath where desired. For the wreath pictured above, we used white azalea blooms.

FLOWER WREATH

Slip a little romance into the season by arranging freeze-dried flowers into an elegant, delicately-hued decoration.

To make the wreath, cover a straw wreath with sheet moss, securing the moss with florist's wire. To make a hanger, form a wire loop and attach it to the back of the wreath.

Cut the stems of the flowers close to the blooms. (The wreath pictured uses roses, hydrangea, gardenias, and peonies.) Hot-glue the blooms and gold-painted pinecones to the wreath, covering the front and inner circle of the wreath and leaving a gap at the center top for the bow. (For bow-making directions, see page 145.) Glue the bow to the wreath, trailing the bow's streamers along the sides of the wreath and securing them with a dot of glue where necessary to form loops. (Wire-edged ribbon is recommended for this bow.) Glue flowers and pinecones across the center of the bow, if desired.

The wreath pictured was made with freeze-dried flowers; however, silk or waxed flowers are suitable substitutes and will stay fresh-looking for years. To wax flowers, see the directions on page 142. For freeze-dried flowers, see Sources on page 154.

GARDENER'S WREATH

Preserve the abundance of the harvest with a wreath that gathers the colors and textures of autumn and infuses them with holiday red.

To make the wreath, tuck the stems of assorted evergreens such as cedar, juniper, and pine into a vine wreath in a random fashion, covering the entire front and inner wreath. (If necessary, wire a florist's pick to stems for added stability.)

To make the hanger, using florist's wire, form a loop and attach it to the back of the wreath.

Referring to the photo, loosely wrap lengths of vine such as grape, honeysuckle, or kudzu around the wreath. Secure the ends by wiring them to florist's picks and tucking the picks into the wreath.

Embellish the wreath by wiring strips of birch bark, bundles of herbs and berries, and feathers in a random fashion around the wreath as desired.

To secure the apples to the wreath, thread florist's wire through small, green apples, and twist the ends of the wire around the wreath form.

To add the narcissus bulbs, use bulbs that have been forced and have approximately 4" to 6" of green foliage. (For tips on forcing bulbs, see page 147.) Rinse the bulbs and roots well, and wire the bulbs to the wreath. Mist the wreath occasionally to keep it fresh. Use florist's wire to attach the bow. For bow-making directions, see page 145.

Note: For herbs and berries, see Sources on page 154.

Petite Rose
Pot Ornament

Petite
Pomegranate
Pot Ornament

A GARDENER'S TREE

Ornaments and garlands of natural materials and silk flowers bring the
life and color of the garden to the Christmas evergreen.

PETITE POT ORNAMENTS

The earth-red tones of dried roses, pomegranates, and
terra-cotta contrast nicely against the tree's rich green.

For each ornament: Pack a 2" terra-cotta pot with
florist's foam. For an easy fit, place the pot facedown on
the foam block, and gently press down until the pot is
filled with foam. Using a knife, slice off the foam level
with the top of the pot.

For the rose pot: Press 3 to 4 small dried roses with stems
into the foam, leaving a small space in the center. For the
hanger, fold an 8" length of raffia in half and knot the
ends together. Using a florist's pin, attach the knotted end
of the raffia to the foam at the center. Press tiny dried
leaf stems into the foam, filling in around the roses and
the hanger.

For the pomegranate pot: Tear off a piece of decorator
moss equal in size to the pot top. Hot-glue the moss to
the foam. Hot-glue half of a florist's pick to the base of a
small, dried pomegranate. Let dry. Press the pomegranate
into the center of the moss. Hot-glue around the edges to
secure the pomegranate. For the hanger, fold an 8" length
of raffia in half and knot the center around the tip of the
pomegranate. Tie the loose ends in a bow.

KISSING BALL

Dried blooms—we used hydrangea and peonies here—add texture and subtle shadings to this classic ornament.

For 1 ornament: Trim the stems of dried flowers to 2". Push the stems into a Styrofoam ball. For fragile stems, first make tiny holes in the foam with an ice pick; then insert the stems, adding a dab of craft glue to secure them, if necessary. Glue petals directly onto the ball, overlapping the edges. Continue until the ball is almost covered, leaving a small uncovered spot to attach the hanger.

For the hanger, fold ¾ yard of 3"-wide sheer ribbon in half and knot the ends together. Using a florist's pin, attach the ribbon to the ball. Hot-glue the ribbon hanger to secure it. Add flowers or petals to fill in around the hanger, as needed.

Note: When selecting a Styrofoam ball, keep in mind that the finished ornament will be approximately twice the size of the original ball. We used a 4" ball for each ornament.

Peony Kissing Ball

CUT AND DRY

To preserve flowers, strip all but the topmost leaves from stems at the peak of blooming, usually late summer. Tie the cuttings into small bundles with twine and hang them upside down in a dark, dry place for at least 3 weeks.

For a quicker drying method, microwave blooms or petals. Place 3 paper towels on a microwave-safe plate. Arrange fresh blooms or petals on top in a single layer and cover them with a paper towel. Microwave on HIGH for 3 minutes. Check for dryness. Replace the paper towels when they become moist. Continue microwaving at 30-second intervals, until the desired dryness is reached.

Hydrangea Kissing Ball

Violet Bouquet

VIOLET BOUQUET

Bundles of silk flowers bring tiny gifts of color.

For 1 bouquet: Hold together 4 dozen silk violets with 5" stems, and evenly arrange 5 silk leaves with wire stems around the flower bouquet. With the right sides of the leaves facing the flowers, wrap the stems together at the center with a small amount of florist's tape.

To make the bow, tie ⅓ yard of 3"-wide sheer ribbon around the tape. Knot the ribbon to secure it. Tuck the bouquet among the tree branches where desired.

BLOOMING BULB ORNAMENT

Whether the blooms are real or silk, they'll bring a fresh look to your tree.

For 1 ornament: Handling the blooms and stems as 1 unit, wrap 2 long-stemmed artificial narcissus blooms and 5 artificial stems onto a florist's pick, using florist's tape and leaving 1½" at the bottom of the pick unwrapped. Tuck the unwrapped portion of the pick into the top of a narcissus bulb as close to the bulb tip as possible. Trim or break off the excess pick. Tuck the blooms deep into the tree branches as desired.

Blooming
Bulb
Ornament

PAILS OF GRASS

A lighter shade of evergreen—brightly-hued ryegrass—
sprouts from shiny, galvanized steel pots.

For 1 pail: Arrange rocks or pebbles in the bottom of a
galvanized pail. In a separate container, fold ryegrass seed
into potting soil. Fill the pail ¾ full with the seeded soil,
and sprinkle a heavy layer of seed on top. Water the soil.

Place the pail in a sunny spot and water it regularly.
The seed will sprout in approximately 10 days. Manicure
the grass with scissors as needed.

To make the holiday markers, if desired, write holiday
greetings on metal garden markers, using a dry-erase pen.
Press the markers into the soil.

Garden Accents Ornaments

Recycle foam food trays into gazebo, urn, and garden gate cutouts for the tree.

For 1 ornament: Using tracing paper, transfer the desired pattern on page 142 to an 8½" x 11" sheet of craft foam, or use clean, foam food trays from the grocery store. Cut out the ornament.

To make the hanger, pierce the ornament at the center top with a pencil tip or other pointed object. Thread an 8" length of thin, gold craft wire through the hole and knot the ends together, forming a hanger.

Gazebo Ornament

Pansy-Chain Garland

This floral garland takes its cue from the daisy chains of childhood.

For a 7' garland: Tie 1 silk pansy with a 5" stem to a second pansy just below the bloom, as if making a daisy chain. Knot the stems to secure. Leaving 4" between blooms, repeat, until you have strung 23 pansies together. Wrap the garland around the tree branches as desired.

Narcissus Bulb Garland

Natural bulbs hint at the promise of spring.

For a 3' garland: Wrap ½ yard of waxed garden cord or floral cord around the tip of 1 narcissus bulb, and tie the cord in a knot. Crisscross the cord around the body of the bulb, wrapping it around the tip and forming a weblike hold. Knot the cord ends. Secure the cord at the top and the bottom of the bulb with florist's pins. Repeat the process, for a total of 12 bulbs.

To form the garland, cut small strips of waxed garden cord and slip them under the florist's pins. Tie the bulbs together from pin to pin. Wind the garland around the tree branches as desired.

Pansy-Chain Garland

Narcissus Bulb Garland

APPLE CHANDELIER

Fruit—especially shiny apples in the season's signature color—makes
a fresh decoration for the dining room chandelier.

small red apples
24-gauge wire
greenery sprigs: eucalyptus, pine
ribbon
red berries on vines or stems

1. To prepare the apples, determine how many apples you
want to hang, keeping in mind the weight of the apples
in relation to the chandelier. Fold 1 (18") length of wire
in half, and push it through each apple from the bottom
to the top.

Place a sprig of eucalyptus and pine at the center top
of each apple, twisting together with wire to secure.
2. Cut the ribbon into 1 (29") length for each apple. Tie
each length in a bow. Wire a bow to each apple over the
greenery.

3. To hang the apples, cut the remaining ribbon into
strips that are twice the desired suspension length for
each plus 6". Referring to the photograph, wrap each ribbon strip over the top of the chandelier, and tie the ends
in a double knot. Using the same end of the wire that
holds the greenery and bow, wire each apple to the ribbon
hanger at the knot. Push the excess wire back into the
apple to secure and conceal it.
4. Place sprigs of eucalyptus inside the tops of the ribbon
hangers, and entwine vines or stems of berries around the
chandelier as desired.

*Note: To ensure freshness, prepare this arrangement no more
than 10 days ahead of time. Consider using artificial berries;
they work just as well, and the berries won't drop.*

NAPKIN MANTEL SCARF

This neat mantel dressing requires minimal assembly. Choose napkins in your favorite holiday prints and colors.

5 holiday napkins (approximately 18" square)
⅝"-wide fusible bonding web
7 fishing lure swivel hooks
4 yards wire-edged ribbon
7 ornaments

1. To assemble the mantel scarf, overlap the napkins so that the top napkin covers approximately ¼ of the bottom napkin. Pin the napkins in place. Repeat until all of the napkins are pinned together. Adjust the number of napkins or vary the amount of overlap to achieve the correct length for your mantel, if necessary. To ensure that the points are even, measure the exposed edges and check for equal lengths. Adjust and repin if necessary.

2. Following manufacturer's directions, fuse the napkins together along the overlapped edges. Repeat the fusing procedure on the wrong side of the mantel scarf.

3. To attach the ornaments, sew the "eye" of a swivel hook to each napkin point that will hold an ornament, including the points at each end of the scarf. Open the hook. Cut a 20" length of ribbon for each ornament. Tie each ribbon into a bow. Slide the swivel hook through the back side of the bow. Position the scarf on the mantel; attach the ornaments.

Note: The mantel scarf is approximately 5' long. Swivel hooks are available in sporting goods stores and the sporting goods section of most discount stores.

THE GIFT OF VELVET

These festive pillows wrap up the color and
comfort of the season.

For 1 pillow:

⅝ yard (45"-wide) plaid acetate crinkle fabric

3½ yards cording

⅔ yard velvet

1 (20-ounce) bag polyester stuffing

1. To make the "ribbon," from the plaid fabric, cut the
following bias strips: 4"-wide strips totaling 2 yards; 2
(4½" x 24") strips for the ties.

Fold under 1" along each long edge of the 4"-wide bias
strip, having raw edges meet in the center. Press. Cut the
bias strip into 7 (10") lengths. Notch the center of the
strips at each end.

2. To make the piping, from the plaid fabric, cut 1½"-
wide bias strips totaling 3⅓ yards. With wrong sides facing and raw edges aligned, wrap the bias strips around the
cording and machine-baste, using a cording foot or a zipper foot. Piece the strips where necessary. Each pillow
requires 4 (10"-long) pieces and 2 (approximately 36"-
long) pieces.

3. To make the pillows, from velvet, cut 6 (10" x 10")
squares.

4. To make the pillow sides, notch the center point of the
top and bottom of 4 velvet squares. With right sides facing up, baste a plaid strip (from Step 1) to each of the 4
squares, matching centers.

Machine-baste 1 (10"-long) section of piping to 1 edge
of a side piece, aligning the raw edges of the piping and
the velvet. (To reduce bulk, trim the cording ⅝" from the
ends.) With the nap running in the same direction, sew
the 2 sides together. Repeat sewing the piping and sides
together until 3 side seams have been sewn.

Machine-baste the 36"-long pieces of piping to the top
and bottom of the side section, trimming the cording
from the seam allowance.

Stitch the fourth seam of the side section. Make center
notches on all edges of both the top and bottom squares.

5. To make the pillow bottom, baste 2 bias strips (from
Step 1) to a velvet square, matching notches. With right
sides facing, hand-baste the pillow bottom to the side section, matching center notches and leaving a 6" section
open for turning. With the side section on top, stitch on
top of the previous stitching, pivoting at the corner
seams. Leave a 6" section open for turning.

6. To make the pillow top, baste 1 bias strip (from Step 1)
to a velvet square. Make the ties by folding the 4½" x 24"
bias strips, right sides together. Using a ¼" seam allowance, stitch the long edge, leaving 1 end open and
angling the other end. Trim the excess, turn, and press.
Notch the center of the tie raw edge. Baste the ties to the
pillow top, matching center notches.

With right sides facing, hand-baste the pillow top to
the side section, matching centers. With the side section
on top, stitch on top of the previous stitching, pivoting at
the corner seams. Turn the pillow. Fill it with polyester
stuffing; stitch the opening closed. Tie a bow at the top of
the pillow.

*Note: Pillow measures 9⅜" square. All seams are ⅝" unless
otherwise noted.*

SHAPES OF THE SEASON

These topiaries—scented with dried lavender and rose petals,
fir needles and cloves—prettily accent sideboards and mantels.

FIR TREE TOPIARY

10" Styrofoam cone

spruce green acrylic spray paint (or green cone)

Styrofoam ball to fit top of pot

rust-colored acrylic spray paint

clay pot

white glue

¼"-diameter dowel

hot-glue gun and glue sticks

2 to 3 cups dried Frasier fir needles

¼ cup dried lavender buds

powdered cinnamon

broken cinnamon sticks

allspice berries

whole cloves

2 star anise stars

1. To prepare the cone, paint it green or use a green cone. Cut the Styrofoam ball in half and paint 1 half rust. Let dry. Wedge the half-ball into the pot, and secure it with glue. Cut a length of dowel 2" to 3" longer than the desired trunk length. Slip the dowel in the center bottom of the cone to form the trunk of the tree, securing it with hot glue.

2. To cover the cone, strip 2 to 3 cups of fir needles from dried branches. (Cuttings from a Christmas tree are ideal.) Mix fir needles with ¼ cup of lavender buds. Coat the cone with a thick layer of white glue, and roll the cone in the potpourri mixture to adhere the mixture to the cone. Press clumps of potpourri firmly into any bare areas. Let dry. If any bare spots remain, touch the spots with a dab of glue, then cover them with lavender buds.

3. To cover the half-ball, coat it with glue, then roll it in powdered cinnamon. Let dry. Cover it with a mosaic of broken cinnamon sticks and whole spices, gluing the pieces on separately. Let dry.

4. To attach the tree to the pot, place the bottom end of the dowel in the center top of the spice-covered half-ball, securing it with hot glue. Glue 2 star anise stars together, back-to-back, and glue them to the top of the tree.

LAVENDER & ROSE TOPIARY

large cookie cutter in desired shape

½"-thick sheet Styrofoam

¼"-diameter dowel

low-temperature glue gun and glue sticks

3"-diameter Styrofoam ball

lavender acrylic craft paint

4"-diameter clay pot

dried rose petals and lavender buds

white glue

1. To create the shape, use a cookie cutter to cut the desired shape from Styrofoam. Press the edges with fingers to round and smooth the shape. Cut a 4¼" length of dowel. Slip the dowel in the base of the cookie-cutter shape to a depth of about 1", securing it with glue.

2. To form the base, cut the Styrofoam ball in half. Paint the rounded surface of the half-ball with lavender paint. Let dry. Wedge the half-ball, curved side up, in the pot. Secure it with glue. Paint the backs of the dried rose petals with glue (one at a time) and press them onto the Styrofoam cookie-cutter shape, covering it with a mosaic of petals. Leave a few small skips in the petal mosaic. Paint the skips with glue, and press clumps of lavender into the skips to secure. Let dry.

Press the dowel into the top of the ball in the pot to a depth of 1", securing it with glue. Coat the surface of the ball with white glue. Press the lavender buds firmly onto the glue, covering the exposed surface completely. Let dry.

Lavender &
Rose Topiary

Fir Tree
Topiary

TABLECLOTH TREE SKIRT

Create this bright skirt using two square tablecloths
and a no-sew technique.

diagrams on page 152
2 (52" square) tablecloths
4 yards (17"-wide) paper-backed fusible web
low-temperature glue gun and glue sticks
7 yards trim
8 tassel medallions or individual tassels
Velcro dots (optional)

1. To prepare the tablecloths, wash and dry the tablecloths according to manufacturer's directions. Press. Lay 1 cloth out flat. Lay the second cloth on top of the first, shifting the corners to form an 8-point star shape. (See Diagram 1 on page 152.)

2. To form the tree skirt, cut 1 piece of fusible web the size of the tree skirt center where the cloths overlap. Following manufacturer's directions, fuse the tablecloths together.

3. To cut the opening for the tree trunk, fold the star shape in quarters, aligning the edges, to find the center. Cut a 4"-diameter hole at the center for the trunk of the tree. Cut from the trunk opening to the edge of the star at the V-shaped space between the 2 star points. The fused edges will not ravel. (See Diagram 2 on page 152.)

4. To add the trim, lay the tree skirt out flat. Place the trim along the hemmed edges of the cloth, concealing the stitching. Using a glue gun, apply the trim to the fabric. Press the trim firmly into the glue to secure. Glue a tassel medallion or a tassel to each star point.

5. To fasten the tree skirt, glue Velcro dots to the opening edges if desired. (Washing the tree skirt is not recommended. Spot-clean only.)

EASY EMBELLISHED ORNAMENTS

Ribbon, cording, and tassels personalize shiny, purchased balls.

Ribbon-Wrapped Ornament

Paisley Loop Ornament

PAISLEY LOOP ORNAMENT

For a 5" glass ornament, collect 6 (5½") lengths of colored cording. Seal the ends of the cording with liquid ravel preventer. Handling 3 strands as 1 unit and using a low-temperature glue gun, glue the cording to the ornament in a paisley shape. Repeat as desired.

RIBBON-WRAPPED ORNAMENT

Randomly wrap ⅛"-wide grosgrain ribbon around a glass ornament. To make wrapping easier, dab glue from a low-temperature glue gun on one end of the ribbon, and attach it to the bottom of the ornament. Continue to glue as needed. Glue a purchased tassel to the bottom.

27

HOLLY DOOR CHIMES

A festive greeting for a front or back entrance.

patterns on page 148

tracing paper

posterboard

felt: dark green, medium green, light green

glue stick

craft glue

red jingle bells: 6 (½"), 6 (¾"), 2 (⅜"), 1 (2")

   (Bells can be painted with flat red spray paint.)

¼ yard (¼"-wide) green grosgrain ribbon

1. To make the backing, trace Pattern 1 (entire pattern). Using the pattern, cut 1 backing piece from the poster-board and 1 from the dark green felt. Using a glue stick, glue the posterboard and the dark green felt together.

2. To make the large leaves, using Pattern 2 (light green), cut the larger leaf shapes from light green felt. With craft glue, glue the leaves into place on top of the dark green felt, referring to the photograph for positioning.

3. To make the small leaves, using Pattern 3 (medium green), cut the smaller leaf shapes from medium green felt. With craft glue, glue the leaves into place on top of the light green felt leaves, referring to the photograph for positioning. Leave the edges loose to create texture.

4. To add the bells, referring to the photograph, stitch or glue the jingle bells into place. Fold the ribbon in half, and stitch or glue to the point of the holly at the bottom of the chimes. Thread the ribbon ends through the remaining bells and tie them in a bow.

MONOGRAMMED STOCKING

This fancy-looking velvet-and-lace stocking is a cinch to stitch.

pattern on page 146

tracing paper

½ yard velvet

½ yard lining fabric

½ yard 3½"-wide single-edged lace

½ yard ½"-wide single-edged lace (Adjust amount to
customize your initials, if necessary.)

liquid ravel preventer

1. To cut out the stocking, trace the pattern onto tracing paper, extending the lines at the ankle 8". For the stocking front and back, with right sides facing and raw edges aligned, place the pattern on folded velvet. Cut out the stocking. For the stocking lining front and back, with right sides facing and raw edges aligned, place the pattern on folded lining fabric. Cut out the lining. For the cuff, cut 1 (17") length of 3½"-wide lace.

2. To form the letters, cut 2" lengths of ½"-wide lace, and overlap them to form the desired letters. Seal the cut edges of the lace with liquid ravel preventer. Slipstitch or machine-stitch the letters in the desired positions on the stocking front.

3. To make the hanging loop, cut 1 (2" x 4") strip from the lining fabric. With right sides facing and raw edges aligned, fold the strip in half lengthwise, and stitch the long edges together; turn. Fold the hanger in half to make a loop.

4. To assemble the stocking, with right sides facing and raw edges aligned, stitch the velvet stocking pieces together, leaving the top open. Trim the seams, and turn the stocking right side out. With the raw edges aligned, baste the hanger to the outside of the stocking at the back seam.

With right sides facing and raw edges aligned, stitch the lining pieces together, leaving the top open and a 6" opening on the straight side for turning. Trim the seams. Do not turn the lining. With right sides facing, raw top edges aligned, and side seams matching, stitch the lining to the stocking at the top, sandwiching the hanging loop

in the seam. Turn the lining to the inside. Slipstitch the opening closed.

5. To make the cuff, with right sides facing and raw edges aligned, stitch the cuff side seam. Aligning the top of the cuff and the top of the stocking, slipstitch or edgestitch the lace cuff to the stocking.

BY THE CHIMNEY WITH CARE

These bright, elfin-toed stockings add color and whimsy to your mantel.

Velvet &
Brocade Stocking

VELVET & BROCADE STOCKING

patterns and diagram on page 149

graph paper with 1" grid (optional)

½ yard brocade

⅔ yard velvet

⅔ yard trim (or decorative cording with flange)

2 (2") tassels

VELVET & FRINGE STOCKING

patterns and diagram on page 149

graph paper with 1" grid (optional)

½ yard taupe velvet

½ yard black velvet

⅝ yard 2½"-wide fringe

Note: All seams ⅝" unless otherwise noted.

For the Velvet & Brocade Stocking:

1. To cut out the stocking, using graph paper and the stocking patterns, enlarge the patterns; or enlarge the patterns on a photocopier, if desired. Using the patterns, cut the stocking front and toe pieces from brocade. Cut the front inset and 1 whole stocking for the stocking back from velvet. Using the cuff pattern, cut 2 cuffs on the fold from black velvet. For the hanger, cut a 1¼" x 10" bias strip from black velvet.

2. To make the stocking front, sew the stocking front piece to the stocking inset at the inside seams. Sew the front piece/inset to the toe at the inside seam. Clip, trim, and press the seams toward the brocade, using a pressing cloth to protect the nap of the velvet.

3. To assemble the stocking, with right sides facing and raw edges aligned, pin and sew the front to the back, leaving the top open. Trim the seams, and clip the curves. Turn the stocking right side out.

4. To add the trim to the cuff, pin the edge of the trim to the right side of 1 cuff along the raw edge. Baste the trim in place. Do not cut the excess trim at this time. Using a zipper foot, sew the cuff facing to the cuff across the bottom edge, with the trim edge sandwiched in between. Pivot at the center point. Clip to the stitching at the center point; trim the seam.

Secure the trim and tassels in place at the side edges by stitching along the seam line, keeping tassels free; stitch again ½" from the raw edge. Cut the trim close to the second line of stitches.

For the Velvet & Fringe Stocking:

1. To cut out the stocking, using graph paper and the stocking pattern, enlarge the pattern; or enlarge the pattern on a photocopier, if desired. For the stocking front and back, with right sides facing and raw edges aligned, place the pattern on the folded taupe velvet. Cut out the stocking. Using the pattern, cut 2 cuffs on the fold from black velvet. (One will be used for a self facing.) For the

Velvet & Fringe Stocking

hanger, cut a 1¼" x 10" bias strip from black velvet.

With right sides facing and raw edges aligned, sew the stocking sections together, leaving the top open. Trim the seams, and clip the curves.

2. To add the fringe to the cuff, measure 1⅝" from the cut edge of the bottom of 1 cuff piece; pin the top of the fringe in place along this "line." Sew the fringe in place, stitching only along the top edge of the fringe. Do not trim the excess fringe at this time.

Folding the fringe up and out of the way, sew the cuff facing to the cuff across the bottom edge, pivoting at the center point. Clip to the stitching at the center point; trim the seam. Secure the fringe in place at the side edges by stitching along the seam line; stitch again ½" from the raw edge. Trim the fringe close to the second line of stitches.

For Both Stockings:

1. To make the cuff, with right sides facing and with seams and raw edges aligned, sew the cuff to the cuff facing at the sides (see diagram), leaving the ends open. Trim the seam. Turn the cuff right side out. Baste the top raw edges together.

Pin the cuff to the stocking, with the cuff facing to the stocking right side. Ease the cuff to fit the stocking; pin, matching side seams. Baste in place.

2. To make the hanger, fold the bias strip in half lengthwise. Stitch with ¼" seam allowance. Turn. Trim to an 8½" length. Baste the ends of the hanging loop in place at the back of the stocking, keeping the raw edges aligned.

3. To finish the stocking, sew the cuff and hanging loop to the stocking. Pin the seam toward the inside of the stocking. Edgestitch the seam, keeping the cuff free.

33

HEIRLOOM CHRISTMAS ANGEL

This vision in lace and ribbon symbolizes the grace of the season.
Amazingly, creating this angel requires no special artistry—just
patience in waiting for the glue to dry.

patterns on pages 143-145

10" square flesh-colored nylon
1 yard (45"-wide) bridal fabric
1½ yards nylon tulle
⅓ yard metallic gold lining
3 yards (6"- to 12"-wide) double-edge scalloped bridal lace

small amount (2 handfuls) polyester stuffing
1 package fusible bonding web (We used Stitch Witchery®.)
1 package rayon seam tape

doll head and arms with hands (for 14" doll)
large acrylic doll cone (or small sheet flexible craft acrylic)

hot-glue gun and glue sticks
craft glue (We used Sobo.)
heavy-duty glue (We used E-6000®.)

thin craft wire
48" length white-coated doorbell wire (available at
    hardware stores)

1 package 16-gauge brass wire
3 yards gold metallic twine

5½ yards 3"-wide gold wire-edged ribbon
6 yards 1½"-wide gold-and-ivory wire-edged ribbon
2¼ yards 2"-wide wire-edged ivory ribbon
2 yards 3"-wide gold mesh wire-edged ribbon
6 yards 1½"-wide wire-edged gold crinkle-textured ribbon
6 yards 2"-wide ivory ribbon
3½ yards ⅛"-wide gold-and-ivory ribbon
4 yards ⅝"-wide white braid
1 yard ⅝"-wide gold-and-white scalloped braid
5½ yards ¼"-wide gold-and-white scalloped braid
2 yards ¼"-wide white braid

4 yards 4-mm gold-and-white cording
3 yards 2-mm gold-and-white cording

14" length plastic pearls-by-the-yard
10" length rhinestones-by-the-yard
3½"- to 4"-tall brush Christmas tree
15-mm star charm

ARMS, BODY, AND HEAD ASSEMBLY

Arms and Hands:

From the 10" flesh-colored fabric square, cut 1 (7¾" x 2 ¾") rectangle. With the fabric on a flat surface, lay the doll arms on each end of the fabric, placing the arms ¼" inside the ends of the fabric. Fill in the space between the arms with a handful of polyester stuffing; hot-glue the fabric around the elbows. Using craft glue, glue the fabric edges together into a roll, forming one long tube with hands at each end. Use pins to hold the roll in place while gluing, if necessary. ▼

Torso:

Place the remaining fabric from the 10" flesh-colored square on a flat surface. Place a handful of polyester stuffing in the center. Pull the fabric up around the stuffing, and secure it with a short length of craft wire, forming a ball. Trim the excess fabric. ▶

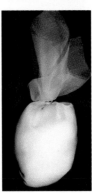

Body:

Lay the arm roll across the top of the torso "ball," positioning it evenly so the arm lengths are equal. Hot-glue the arm roll in place (A).

Head and Shoulders:

Position the head and shoulders over the arms/torso. Check the alignment and straighten, if necessary. Hot-glue the head in place (B).

CONE BASE AND BODY ASSEMBLY

Cone Base:

If a large acrylic doll cone is unavailable, use the cone pattern to cut a cone from a sheet of flexible craft acrylic. Cut vent holes as indicated on the pattern. Tape the cone together and staple it to hold the shape in place.

Cone and Body:

Fit the body into the hole at the top of the cone base. (You may need to trim the hole, but the body should fit tightly, so don't trim too much.) Pull and adjust the body to form a bust line and waistline. Hot-glue the body in place, being careful not to melt the acrylic (C).

PETTICOAT ASSEMBLY

Petticoats:

Cut 2 (45" x 11½") rectangles of nylon tulle. Lay 1 tulle rectangle on a flat surface. Pin 1 (45" length) of 3"-wide gold wire-edged ribbon along the bottom edge of the tulle. Zigzag the ribbon to the tulle on both sides. Just above the first row, pin and zigzag 1 (45" length) of 1½"-wide gold-and-ivory wire-edged ribbon. Above the second row, pin and zigzag 1 (45" length) of ⅝"-wide white braid. Pin and zigzag 1 (45" length) of scalloped braid to the bottom of the hemline. Stitch or glue the back seams of the ribbon-trimmed

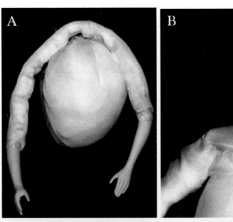

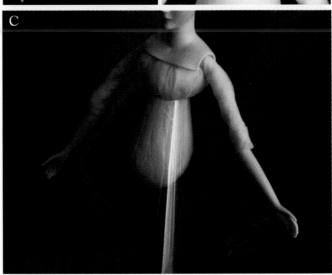

petticoat and the tulle petticoat. Place the tulle petticoat inside the ribbon-trimmed petticoat, aligning the raw edges at the waistline. Gather the waistline of both petticoats at the same time. (To gather, stitch 2 rows of gathering threads along the waistline edge and draw them up.) The gathered waistline is approximately 10".

Petticoat Attachment:
Drop the petticoats over the angel's head. Pull the seams to the back, and adjust and pin the waistline to fit. Hot-glue the petticoats to the waistline to secure them. ▶

SKIRT ASSEMBLY AND TRIM
Skirt:
Cut 1 (45" x 20") rectangle from bridal fabric and 1 (45" x 20") rectangle from nylon tulle. Glue the tulle skirt piece to the wrong side of the bridal fabric skirt piece. Let dry. (From this point, the bridal fabric skirt and the tulle lining will be treated as one unit.) On the wrong side of the skirt, mark a 3½" hem with a fabric marking pencil.

Wire Attachment:
Using your hands, straighten a 48" length of white-coated doorbell wire. (The wire shapes the skirt bottom.) With the skirt fabric right side down, pin strips of fusible web ¼" below the marked hemline. Place the doorbell wire on top of the fusible web; pin in place. Place the seam tape over the wire, and pin it to secure. With the skirt fabric right side down, following manufacturer's directions, fuse the wire to the hem and seam tape, removing the pins as you go.

Skirt Hem:
With the skirt fabric right side down, fold up the hem on the marked line. Fold under ¼" on the top raw edge; pin in place. Steam-press the fabric lightly to crease the hemline and top fold. Remove the pins, and slide a strip of fusible web between the skirt and the hem. Repin if necessary. Following manufacturer's directions, fuse the hem, removing the pins as you go.

Hem Trim:
Cut a 45" length of scalloped-edge lace. Place the lace on the skirt so the bottom edge falls just below the hemline. Attach the lace with craft glue.

Sew, fuse, or glue the back seam of the skirt. Twist the doorbell wire together, trimming the excess wire. Slide the skirt on the body. Adjust it to fit at the waist; pin and glue it in place.

BODICE, WAIST, AND ARM RIBBONS
Bodice:
Using the bodice pattern, cut the bodice from bridal fabric. Drop the bodice over the head, trimming the neckline, if necessary, to fit; pin the arm and side seams. Trim the excess fabric at the waist. Glue the arm and side seams. Let dry. ▼

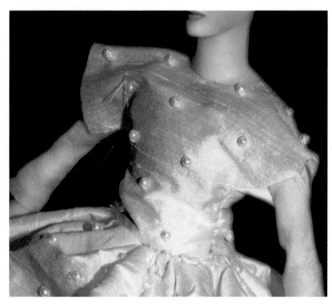

Waist Ribbon:

Measure the waist and add ½". Cut 1 piece of 1½"-wide gold-and-ivory wire-edged ribbon to that measurement. Wrap the ribbon around the waist, pinning it together in the back with the raw edge folded under. Glue the ribbon in place. Let dry. ▶

Arm Ribbon:

Cut the following ribbons: 2 (2") lengths of 2"-wide ivory wire-edged ribbon; 2 (2") lengths of 1½"-wide gold-and-ivory wire-edged ribbon.

Run a line of hot glue from the elbow to the wrist, and attach the ivory wire-edged ribbon, wrapping the ribbon around the arm and folding the raw edges under. Glue the ribbon in place. Let dry. Use a clothespin or clip to hold the ribbon in place until dry.

Beginning at the back of the elbow, run a line of hot glue to the shoulder. Wrap the gold-and-ivory wire-edged ribbon around the upper arm, slightly overlapping the ribbon at the elbow and shoulder, and folding the raw edges under. Glue the ribbon in place. Let dry. Use a clothespin or clip to hold the ribbon in place until dry. ▶

OVERSKIRT

Lace Drape:

Cut a 30" length of scalloped lace. With the angel facing you, pin 1 end of the lace under the right arm at the waist. Drape the lace around the skirt, and pin the other end at the same point. Glue in place. Let dry.

Bouffant Drape:

Lift the skirt fabric up and slightly over the draped lace all around the skirt. Pin or clip the fabric in place to create the desired bouffant appearance. When satisfied with the look, glue the fabric in place. Let dry.

Appliqués:

Cut 4 to 6 appliqués from the lace. Glue the appliqués into the skirt folds in a random pattern. Let dry.

SLEEVES

Sleeve Construction:

Using the sleeve pattern, cut 2 sleeves from bridal fabric and 2 from the gold lining. Place the sleeve fabric right side down on a flat surface. Pin the fusible web around all edges. Place the lining on top of the sleeve fabric; pin in place. Following manufacturer's directions, fuse the lining to the sleeve, removing pins as you go. Pin the sleeve seams together between the marks indicated on the pattern. Zigzag, glue, or fuse the seams closed.

Sleeve Lining Trim:

To trim the sleeve lining edge, cut 2 (18") lengths of 4-mm cording and 4 (18") lengths of ⅛"-wide white braid. Measure 1" up from the bottom of the sleeve lining. Beginning at the seam line, glue the cording along the 1" line to cover the raw sleeve edge. Let dry. Glue the braid just above the cording. Let dry.

Sleeve Trim:

Turn the sleeves to the right side. Cut 2 (18") lengths of scalloped-edge lace. Beginning at the sleeve seam, glue the lace along the outside bottom edge of the sleeve, positioning the scallops to fall just below the sleeve edge. Let dry.

Sleeve Attachment:

Slide the sleeve over the arm and up to the shoulder. Turn under the raw edges at the top of the sleeve; pin in place at the shoulder. Using a wooden skewer and craft glue, work the glue between the bodice and the sleeve. Let dry. Remove the pins.

ARM POSITIONING

Turn the palms of the hands to a position to hold the tree and the star. Using a clothespin, clip the wrist and the sleeve edge together. Hot-glue in place. Let dry.

Lift the hands into the desired position. Pin the resulting sleeve folds in place (this will help keep the arms in position). Using a wooden skewer and craft glue, work the glue into the folds until the arms stay in position (this can take several tries). Let dry. Remove the pins and clothespins.

NECK AND SHOULDER CORDING

Cut a short length of scalloped lace and glue it across the back neckline from shoulder to shoulder to cover the raw edges (A). Cut 2⅓ yards each of 2-mm and 4-mm cording. Working from the back of the angel, lift the right arm and sleeve. Holding 1 end of each length of cording together, hot-glue the cording under the arm on the bodice side seam. Let dry.

Wrap the cording up and over the shoulder then under the right arm. Continue wrapping the cording up the side of the sleeve and around the front of the neck and over the left shoulder. Continue down and under the left sleeve, and then over the left shoulder. Pin in place (B). Let the cording drop to the waistline, and pin it in place. Using a wooden skewer and craft glue and starting at the beginning of the cording wrap, dot glue under and between the cords to secure them. Glue the cording at the waist. Let dry.

With the cording hanging from the waistline, make a large loop of cording to hang below the skirt hemline, allowing for cording streamers. Make a knot in the cording where the loop will be attached at the waist. Pin, and hot-glue in place (C). Let dry.

BEADED CAP

Cap Construction:

Cut 1 or more appliqués from the scalloped-edge lace and arrange them to cover the crown of the head. Hot-glue the cap in place. Let dry. ▶

Cap Trim:

Measure around the base of the cap. Cut 2-mm cording, ¼"-wide braid, and a strand of pearls slightly longer than that measurement. Knot each end of the strand of pearls, leaving about 2" on each end.

With a small paintbrush, brush craft glue on the head around the base of the cap. Affix the 2-mm cording around the head, beginning at the back and aligning the cording close to the cap. Let dry. Hot-glue the strand of pearls in place just below the cording. Gently press the pearls in place. Let dry. Trim the excess. Using craft glue, glue ¼"-wide braid in place just under the pearls and around the face. Let dry.

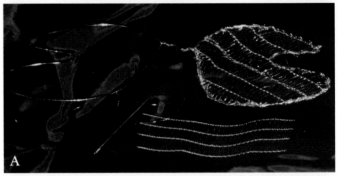

A

WINGS

Wing Construction:

Using the wing pattern, bend the 16-gauge brass wire along the pattern outline, creating the wing frame. Make 2. Leave enough wire on each end to twist the wings together with needle-nose pliers.

Cut 2 (6") lengths of 3"-wide gold mesh wire ribbon. Lay 1 length across each wire wing; hot-glue in place. Let dry. Trim the excess ribbon (A).

Wing Trim:

Cut 2 (18") lengths of ⅝"-wide gold-and-white scalloped braid. Starting at the back of the wing, glue the braid around the outside edge of the wings with scallops facing out. Clip the braid in place to hold it, if necessary (B). Let dry.

Cut 4 (8") lengths of the following: scalloped-edge lace, ⅝"-wide white braid, and ¼"-wide white braid. Glue the lace to the inside of the upper wing, overlapping the gold braid. Let dry. On the lower wing, glue the ⅝"-wide braid around the inside, overlapping the gold braid. Let dry. Glue the ¼"-wide white braid alongside the ⅝"-wide braid (C). Let dry. Glue 4 to 8 scalloped lace appliqués across the middle of the wing. Let dry.

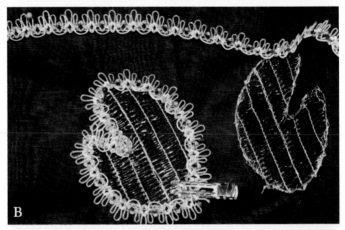

B

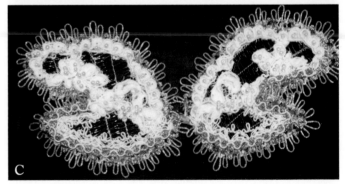

C

Wing Attachment:

Position and pin the wings in the center of the angel back. Hot-glue the wings in place. Let dry.

BACK BOWS

Bow Assembly:

Cut 6 (10") lengths of 1½"-wide gold wire-edged crinkle-textured ribbon and 3 (10") lengths of 2"-wide ivory ribbon. Stack 3 sets of ribbons in the following order: gold crinkle-textured ribbon, ivory ribbon, gold crinkle-textured ribbon. Take 1 stack of ribbons and make a loop, matching the raw ends. Secure the loops at the ends with craft wire, and trim the excess. Repeat to make 2 more ribbon loops. Shape and fluff the loops.

Bow Attachment:

Hot-glue the bows to the back of the angel in a triangular pattern, placing 2 at the center back waistline and 1 in the center just above the 2 waistline bows. Let dry. Fluff and adjust the bows.

HALO

Halo Construction:

Cut 1 (10") length of 16-gauge brass wire. Wrap the wire around a glass jar the size of a baby food jar. Twist the wire together with needle-nose pliers. Leave the wire around the jar for the next 2 steps.

Halo Trim:

Using a wooden skewer, apply a thin coat of heavy-duty glue over the outside of the wire ring. Beginning at the back near the wire twist, glue a strand of rhinestones around the wire. Let dry. Trim the excess rhinestones. Using a wooden skewer, apply a thin line of heavy-duty glue to the top of the rhinestone band. Press gold twine into the glue and against the top of the rhinestone circle. Let dry.

Halo Attachment:

Remove the halo from the jar. (If the glue has adhered to the jar, use a sharp needle to loosen it.) Using wire cutters, trim away any excess wire at the back of the halo. Place the back of the halo under the cap back. Tilt the halo at an angle; hot-glue it in place. Let dry. Using heavy-duty glue, affix an extra rhinestone at the back of the head to cover the gap where the excess wire was removed. Let dry.

FINISHING TOUCHES

RIBBON STREAMERS:

Cut 3 each of the following: 1¼ yards of ¼"-wide white braid, 1 yard of ⅛"-wide gold-and-ivory ribbon, 1⅓ yards gold twine.

Take 1 strand of each ribbon, matching 1 raw end from each. Holding the matched ends, form a 9" loop. Secure the loop with a small piece of wire. Repeat to form loops from the remaining ribbons. The streamers will be uneven.

Cut in half the remaining lengths of ribbon: 2"-wide ivory ribbon, gold-and-ivory wire-edged ribbon, and gold crinkle-textured ribbon. Match the raw ends of each ribbon, pinching them together and securing with a small piece of wire.

Hot-glue the ribbon streamers at the waistline just under the bows. Let dry.

Cut 2 yards each of the gold twine and the ⅛"-wide gold-and-ivory ribbon. Referring to the photograph, drape the twine and ribbon across and over both hands. Pull the streamers down unevenly over the skirt front to form a drape. Hot-glue the streamers in both hands. Let dry.

TREE:

Using wire cutters, trim off the tree base stand. Place the tree in the right hand and hot-glue it to secure. Let dry. Cut 1 (20") length each of gold twine and ⅛"-wide gold-and-ivory ribbon. Tie the twine and ribbon around the right hand, and then tie them together into a bow in front of the tree. Hot-glue in place. Let dry.

STAR:

Put a drop of heavy-duty glue in the palm of the left hand. Press the point of the star charm into the glue. Pull the streamers glued to the left palm around the hand and across the glue and star point. Press the streamers into the glue to secure. Let dry.

ALL THE TRIMMINGS

CHRISTMAS EVE CASSEROLES

Assemble one or two of these savory make-ahead casseroles to serve
when you're busy baking the Christmas Day feast.

You can prepare the dish on the 23rd (when there are still a few minutes to spare), refrigerate it overnight, and pop it in the oven to bake for a great-tasting, no-fuss Christmas Eve dinner. We recommend letting the casseroles stand at room temperature for 30 minutes before baking to take the chill off and to promote even baking. But you can skip this step if you're in a real pinch for time.

CHUNKY HAM POT PIE

Feed a hungry throng with this pot pie brimming with ham, veggies, and Cheddar cheese.

2   tablespoons butter or margarine
1   cup chopped onion
1   (10-ounce) package frozen cut broccoli or flowerets
1   pound new potatoes, coarsely chopped
1   (10¾-ounce) can cream of potato soup, undiluted
1   (8-ounce) carton sour cream
1   cup (4 ounces) shredded sharp Cheddar cheese
¾   cup milk
½   teaspoon garlic powder
½   teaspoon salt
¼   teaspoon pepper
2½ cups chopped honey-baked ham or other ham
½   (15-ounce) package refrigerated piecrusts

• **Melt** butter in a large skillet over medium heat; add onion. Cook 10 minutes or until onion is tender and begins to brown, stirring often.
• **Cook** broccoli according to package directions; drain well. Cook chopped potato in boiling water to cover 10 minutes or until barely tender; drain.
• **Combine** soup and next 6 ingredients in a large bowl, stirring well. Stir in onion, broccoli, potato, and ham. Spoon ham mixture into a greased 3½-quart casserole. (If desired, cover and chill overnight. Let stand at room temperature 30 minutes before baking.)

• **Unfold** piecrust onto a lightly floured surface, and press out fold lines. Roll pastry to extend ¾" beyond edges of casserole. Place pastry over ham mixture. Seal edges, and crimp. Cut slits in top to allow steam to escape. Bake, uncovered, at 400° for 45 minutes or until crust is golden. Let stand 10 minutes before serving. **Yield:** 6 to 8 servings.

Note: You can divide this pot pie into two 2-quart dishes. Bake one now, and freeze one for later. You will need the whole package of piecrusts for two casseroles. Top the casserole to be frozen with crust before freezing, but do not cut slits in top until ready to bake. Let frozen casserole stand at room temperature 20 minutes before baking.

GERMAN SAUSAGE BAKE

Beer, brown mustard, and caraway seeds blend with apples and sausage for a hearty entrée.

6   ounces wide egg noodles, uncooked
Vegetable cooking spray
1   pound kielbasa sausage, sliced
½   cup chopped onion
2   Granny Smith apples, peeled and coarsely chopped (about 2 cups)
3   tablespoons butter or margarine
3   tablespoons all-purpose flour
1   (14½-ounce) can chicken broth
¼   cup flat beer
1   tablespoon spicy brown mustard
1   teaspoon caraway seeds
½   teaspoon salt
¼   teaspoon pepper
2   cups (8 ounces) shredded Swiss cheese, divided
1   cup soft, fresh breadcrumbs (such as rye or pumpernickel)
2   tablespoons butter or margarine, melted

German Sausage Bake

• **Cook** noodles according to package directions; drain well, and set aside.

• **Coat** a large skillet with cooking spray; add sausage, and cook over medium-high heat until sausage is browned, stirring often. Add onion; cook 2 minutes, stirring often. Stir in apple; remove from heat, and set aside.

• **Melt** 3 tablespoons butter in a heavy saucepan over low heat; add flour, stirring until smooth. Cook, stirring constantly, 1 minute. Gradually add chicken broth and beer; cook over medium heat, stirring constantly, until thickened and bubbly. Stir in mustard and next 3 ingredients.

• **Layer** half of cooked noodles in a greased 13" x 9" x 2" baking dish. Spoon sausage mixture over noodles; sprinkle

1 cup Swiss cheese over sausage mixture. Top with remaining noodles. Pour sauce over noodles. (If desired, cover and chill overnight. Let stand at room temperature 30 minutes before baking.)

• **Cover** and bake at 350° for 45 minutes or until thoroughly heated. Uncover and sprinkle with remaining 1 cup Swiss cheese. Combine breadcrumbs and 2 tablespoons butter; sprinkle over casserole. Bake 10 more minutes or until cheese melts and breadcrumbs are browned. Serve immediately. **Yield:** 8 servings.

GARLIC WHITE LASAGNA

Easy lasagna? No problem. We use ready-made Alfredo and skip the boiling water: the uncooked noodles soften in the creamy sauce and cook fully as the lasagna bakes. Hot Italian sausage and fresh garlic punch up the flavor.

1½   pounds hot Italian sausage (in casings)
4   large cloves garlic, chopped
1   medium onion, chopped
1   (12-ounce) jar roasted red pepper, drained and
        chopped
½   cup white wine (such as Chardonnay)
1   (10-ounce) package frozen chopped spinach
1   (15-ounce) carton ricotta cheese
½   teaspoon salt
½   teaspoon pepper
1   large egg, lightly beaten
2   (17-ounce) jars creamy Alfredo sauce*
12   lasagna noodles, uncooked
2   (6-ounce) packages sliced mozzarella cheese
1   cup grated or finely shredded refrigerated Parmesan
        cheese

• **Remove** and discard sausage casings. Brown sausage in a large skillet over medium heat, using a wooden spoon to crumble sausage as it cooks.

• **Drain** sausage, reserving 1 tablespoon drippings in skillet. Cook garlic and onion in reserved drippings over medium-high heat until onion is tender. Stir in sausage, chopped red pepper, and wine. Bring to a boil; reduce heat, and simmer, uncovered, 5 minutes or until most of liquid has evaporated.

• **Meanwhile,** cook spinach according to package directions; drain and squeeze between paper towels to remove excess liquid. Combine spinach, ricotta cheese, and next 3 ingredients; stir well.

• **Spread** 1 cup Alfredo sauce in a greased 13" x 9" x 2" baking dish. Top with 4 uncooked noodles. Top with half of spinach mixture and half of sausage mixture. Place 4 slices mozzarella over sausage mixture. Repeat layers, using 1 cup sauce, 4 noodles, remaining spinach mixture, and remaining sausage mixture.

• **Top** with remaining 4 noodles and mozzarella slices. Spread remaining Alfredo sauce over mozzarella cheese. Sprinkle with Parmesan cheese. (If desired, cover and

Garlic White Lasagna

chill overnight. Let stand at room temperature 30 minutes before baking.)

• **Cover** and bake at 350° for 1 hour, uncovering during last 15 minutes of baking. Let stand 15 minutes before serving. **Yield:** 8 servings.

*For creamy Alfredo sauce, we used Five Brothers. If you want to make your own sauce or use another brand, you'll need 3½ cups sauce.

Note: *Look for roasted red pepper in jars on the grocery aisle with pickles and olives.*

ROASTED CHICKEN AND LEEKS WITH SAGE BISCUIT TOPPING

A buttery herbed crust elevates this dish beyond ordinary chicken pot pie.

2	cups thinly sliced leeks
2	cups sliced celery
1	tablespoon butter or margarine, melted
1	(1.8-ounce) package leek soup and recipe mix
2	cups water
1⅓	cups sour cream
4	cups chopped roasted chicken
½	cup cold butter or margarine, cut into pieces
1	cup self-rising flour
2	tablespoons chopped fresh sage
¾	cup milk

• **Cook** leeks and celery in 1 tablespoon butter in a large skillet over medium-high heat, stirring constantly, until tender.

• **Combine** soup mix and water in a saucepan, stirring until smooth; bring to a boil over medium-high heat. Reduce heat; simmer 2 to 4 minutes or until thickened and bubbly. Remove from heat; stir in sour cream.

• **Combine** leek mixture, soup mixture, and chicken; stir well. Spoon mixture into a lightly greased 11" x 7" x 1½" baking dish. (If desired, cover and chill overnight. Remove from refrigerator, and proceed with next step.)

• **Cut** butter into flour with a pastry blender or two knives until mixture is crumbly. Stir in sage. Add milk, stirring just until dry ingredients are moistened (mixture will be lumpy). Gently spread batter over chicken casserole.

• **Bake,** uncovered, at 400° for 35 minutes or until biscuit topping is golden. **Yield:** 6 servings.

Note: *Purchase a large roasted chicken in the grocer's deli or at the meat counter. Most yield 3 to 4 cups, which should be enough for this recipe.*

BEEF AND SPINACH EN CROÛTE

This flaky-topped entrée of spinach and feta cheese takes its cue from the savory Greek pie, spanakopita. Its pastry topping makes our version best when prepared and served the same day.

½	(17¼-ounce) package frozen puff pastry sheets
1	pound ground chuck
1	medium onion, chopped
1	(10-ounce) package frozen creamed spinach, thawed
1	(4-ounce) package feta cheese, crumbled
1	large egg, lightly beaten
1½	teaspoons dried oregano, divided
½	teaspoon fennel seeds

• **Thaw** puff pastry according to package directions.

• **Cook** ground chuck and onion in a large skillet over medium heat until beef is browned, stirring until beef crumbles; drain. Combine beef mixture, spinach, cheese, egg, and 1 teaspoon oregano, stirring well. Spoon mixture into a greased 11" x 7" x 1½" baking dish.

• **Unfold** puff pastry sheet, and sprinkle with remaining ½ teaspoon oregano and fennel seeds. Roll lightly with a rolling pin to press herbs into pastry. Cut or roll pastry to an 11" x 7" rectangle to fit baking dish. Place pastry over dish. Using a sharp knife, score pastry into 6 squares, if desired. Bake, uncovered, at 400° for 35 minutes or until puffed and golden. **Yield:** 6 servings.

Rich Seafood Casserole

BARBECUE BURGER CASSEROLE

This is a great casserole for the kids—actually, for the kid in all of us.

2   pounds ground chuck
1   medium onion, chopped (1 cup)
¾   cup barbecue sauce
¾   cup spicy ketchup
1   tablespoon prepared mustard
1   teaspoon salt
1   teaspoon pepper
1   (8-ounce) package cream cheese, softened
1   (8-ounce) carton sour cream
¾   cup chopped green onions
3   cups hot cooked medium egg noodles
2½ cups (10 ounces) shredded Cheddar or American
       cheese, divided
Garnish: chopped dill pickle or dill pickle relish

• **Cook** ground chuck and onion in a large skillet over medium heat until beef is browned, stirring until beef crumbles. Drain and return to skillet.

• **Add** barbecue sauce and next 4 ingredients to beef mixture. Bring to a boil; cover, reduce heat, and simmer 10 minutes, stirring once.

• **Combine** cream cheese and sour cream, stirring until smooth. Stir in green onions and cooked noodles.

• **Layer** half of noodle mixture in a greased 13" x 9" x 2" baking dish. Top with half of beef mixture. Sprinkle with 1 cup cheese. Top with remaining noodle mixture and remaining beef mixture. (If desired, cover and chill overnight. Let stand at room temperature 30 minutes before baking.)

• **Cover** and bake at 350° for 30 minutes or until thoroughly heated. Uncover and sprinkle with remaining 1½ cups cheese; bake 5 more minutes. Garnish, if desired.
Yield: 8 servings.

RICH SEAFOOD CASSEROLE

Fresh shrimp and scallops come to the table baked in a Swiss cheese and wine sauce. Spoon over rice.

1½ pounds unpeeled large fresh shrimp
1½ cups dry white wine
¼ cup chopped onion
¼ cup fresh parsley sprigs or celery leaves
1 tablespoon butter or margarine
1 teaspoon salt
1 pound bay scallops
3 tablespoons butter or margarine
3 tablespoons all-purpose flour
1 cup half-and-half
½ cup (2 ounces) shredded Swiss cheese
1 tablespoon lemon juice
¾ teaspoon lemon-pepper seasoning
1 (7-ounce) can sliced mushrooms, drained
1 cup soft whole wheat breadcrumbs
¼ cup grated Parmesan cheese
¼ cup sliced almonds
2 tablespoons butter or margarine, melted
Hot cooked rice

• **Peel** and, if desired, devein shrimp; set aside.
• **Combine** wine and next 4 ingredients in a Dutch oven; bring to a boil. Add shrimp and scallops; cook 3 to 5 minutes or until shrimp turn pink. Drain shrimp mixture, reserving ⅔ cup broth.
• **Melt** 3 tablespoons butter in Dutch oven over low heat; add flour, stirring until smooth. Cook, stirring constantly, 1 minute. Gradually add half-and-half; cook over medium heat, stirring constantly, until mixture is thickened and bubbly. Add Swiss cheese, stirring until cheese melts. Gradually stir in reserved ⅔ cup broth, lemon juice, and lemon-pepper seasoning. Stir in shrimp mixture and mushrooms.
• **Spoon** mixture into a lightly greased 11" x 7" x 1½" baking dish. (If desired, cover and chill overnight. Let stand at room temperature 30 minutes before baking.)
• **Cover** and bake at 350° for 40 minutes. Combine breadcrumbs and next 3 ingredients; sprinkle over casserole. Bake, uncovered, 10 minutes. Let stand 10 minutes before serving. Serve over rice. **Yield:** 8 servings.

SPICY PASTA ALFREDO CASSEROLE

Some sassy ingredients—tomatoes and green chiles, artichoke hearts, roasted peppers—team up for a meatless main dish or a rich side to chicken, ham, or beef.

1 (12-ounce) package fettuccine, uncooked
2 (1.6-ounce) packages Alfredo sauce mix*
2 cups milk
1 cup water
2 tablespoons butter or margarine
1 (16-ounce) carton sour cream
1 (10-ounce) can diced tomatoes and green chiles, drained
1 (14-ounce) can quartered artichoke hearts, drained
1 (12-ounce) jar roasted red pepper, drained and chopped
1 cup freshly grated or finely shredded refrigerated Parmesan cheese

• **Cook** pasta according to package directions; drain well. Set aside.
• **Combine** sauce mix and next 3 ingredients in a large saucepan; bring to a boil over medium heat, stirring constantly. Reduce heat; cook, stirring constantly, 2 minutes or until sauce is thickened and bubbly. Stir in sour cream and tomatoes and green chiles.
• **Combine** pasta, sauce mixture, artichokes, and red pepper; spoon mixture into a greased 13" x 9" x 2" baking dish. (If desired, cover and chill overnight. Let stand at room temperature 30 minutes before baking.)
• **Cover** and bake at 350° for 1 hour. Uncover casserole, and sprinkle with cheese; bake, uncovered, 10 more minutes or until cheese is lightly browned. **Yield:** 6 main-dish servings or 10 side-dish servings.

*For Alfredo sauce mix, we used Knorr. Find it near dry gravy mixes and other sauce packets.

SIDEKICKS

The next few pages will inspire you to venture beyond old favorite holiday side dishes. These revised recipes incorporate some unexpected flavors for the season.

Brussels Sprouts au Gratin

BRUSSELS SPROUTS AU GRATIN

This saucy vegetable got our test kitchen's highest rating.

¼   cup fine, dry breadcrumbs

1   tablespoon grated Parmesan cheese

2   pounds fresh brussels sprouts*

2   tablespoons butter or margarine

2   tablespoons all-purpose flour

1½ cups milk

1   cup (4 ounces) shredded Gruyère or Swiss cheese

1   tablespoon white wine Worcestershire sauce

½   teaspoon salt

¼   teaspoon pepper

¼   teaspoon paprika

• **Combine** breadcrumbs and Parmesan cheese; set aside. Wash brussels sprouts; remove discolored leaves. Trim ends, and cut in half lengthwise. Cook sprouts in boiling water to cover 12 minutes or until barely tender. Drain and place in a lightly greased 1½-quart gratin dish or an 11" x 7" x 1½" baking dish. Set aside.

• **Melt** butter in a saucepan over low heat; add flour, stirring until smooth. Cook, stirring constantly, 1 minute. Gradually add milk; cook over medium heat, stirring constantly, until thickened and bubbly.

• **Add** Gruyère cheese and next 3 ingredients, stirring until cheese melts.

• **Spoon** sauce over brussels sprouts; sprinkle with breadcrumb mixture and paprika. Bake, uncovered, at 350° for 20 minutes or until browned and bubbly. **Yield:** 8 servings.

* Substitute three 10-ounce packages frozen brussels sprouts for fresh sprouts, if desired. Prepare according to package directions before assembling the casserole.

Broccoli with Three-Cheese
Horseradish Sauce

Tangy Tomato-Glazed
Green Beans

BROCCOLI WITH THREE-CHEESE HORSERADISH SAUCE

We spike this luxurious sauce with horseradish and a little red pepper.

2   pounds fresh broccoli
1   tablespoon all-purpose flour
1½ cups whipping cream, divided
1   cup (4 ounces) shredded sharp Cheddar cheese
1   cup (4 ounces) shredded Monterey Jack cheese
2   tablespoons grated Asiago or Parmesan cheese
1½ tablespoons prepared horseradish
½   teaspoon salt
¼   to ½ teaspoon ground red pepper

• **Remove** broccoli leaves, and cut off tough ends of stalks; discard. Wash broccoli, and cut into spears. Arrange spears in a steamer basket over boiling water. Cover and steam 8 to 10 minutes or until broccoli is crisp-tender.
• **Combine** flour and ½ cup whipping cream in a saucepan, stirring until smooth. Stir in remaining 1 cup whipping cream. Cook over medium heat, stirring constantly, until thickened and bubbly.
• **Add** Cheddar cheese and remaining 5 ingredients; cook, stirring constantly, until cheeses melt. Spoon sauce over broccoli spears; serve immediately.
Yield: 8 servings.

TANGY TOMATO-GLAZED GREEN BEANS

These beans, covered with a balsamic-brown sugar glaze, are well-matched with ham.

1½ pounds fresh green beans
½   cup balsamic vinegar
½   cup dried tomatoes
6   slices bacon
2   tablespoons minced shallot
2   tablespoons brown sugar
¼   teaspoon salt
⅛   teaspoon pepper

• **Wash** beans; trim ends, and remove strings. Cook beans in boiling water to cover 10 minutes or until crisp-tender. Drain and set aside.
• **Bring** vinegar to a boil in a saucepan; remove from heat. Add tomatoes; let stand 10 minutes. Drain tomatoes, reserving vinegar. Coarsely chop tomatoes.
• **Cook** bacon in a large skillet over medium heat until crisp; remove bacon, reserving 2 tablespoons drippings in skillet. Crumble bacon, and set aside.
• **Cook** shallot in reserved bacon drippings over medium heat, stirring constantly, until tender. Add reserved vinegar, chopped tomato, brown sugar, salt, and pepper. Cook over low heat until sugar melts, stirring occasionally.
• **Add** beans to skillet, and toss gently. Cook just until thoroughly heated. Spoon bean mixture into a serving bowl; sprinkle with bacon. **Yield:** 6 servings.

Spinach and
Artichoke
Timbale

Rosemary-Roasted
Sweet Potatoes

SPINACH AND ARTICHOKE TIMBALES

This rich, molded dish makes a stately side.

1   cup chopped fresh mushrooms
2   tablespoons minced onion
2   tablespoons butter or margarine, melted
1   (14-ounce) can artichoke hearts, drained and
        chopped
1   (10-ounce) package frozen chopped spinach,
        thawed and well drained
1   (3-ounce) package cream cheese, softened
¾   cup half-and-half
2   large eggs
½   cup grated Parmesan-Romano cheese blend
¾   teaspoon lemon-pepper seasoning
⅛   teaspoon dry mustard
Garnish: pimiento strips

• **Cook** mushrooms and onion in butter in a skillet over medium-high heat until tender, stirring occasionally. Combine mushroom mixture, chopped artichoke, and spinach in a large bowl.
• **Beat** cream cheese at medium speed of an electric mixer until creamy. Gradually add half-and-half, beating until smooth. Add eggs and next 3 ingredients; beat mixture just until blended. Add to spinach mixture; stir well.
• **Spoon** mixture into six 6-ounce lightly greased timbale molds or custard cups. Place molds in a shallow baking dish; add hot water to dish to depth of 1".

• **Bake** at 350° for 43 to 45 minutes or until set. Remove from water; cool 5 minutes before unmolding. Loosen edges of timbales with a spatula or small knife; invert onto a serving plate. Garnish, if desired. **Yield:** 6 servings.

ROSEMARY-ROASTED SWEET POTATOES

These wedges caramelize naturally while they roast. They look and taste great with ham, turkey, or beef.

2   large sweet potatoes
⅓   cup butter or margarine, melted
¼   cup firmly packed brown sugar
1   tablespoon chopped fresh or dried rosemary
2   teaspoons grated orange rind
½   teaspoon kosher salt
Garnish: fresh rosemary

• **Peel** potatoes, if desired. Cut each potato in half crosswise; cut each half into 8 wedges.
• **Combine** butter and next 4 ingredients in a large heavy-duty, zip-top plastic bag; add potato wedges. Seal bag, and shake until potato wedges are well coated. Arrange wedges in a greased roasting pan or jellyroll pan.
• **Bake** at 400° for 40 minutes or until potato wedges are tender and browned, stirring occasionally. Garnish, if desired. **Yield:** 4 servings.

SCALLOPED NEW POTATOES AND LEEKS

A stocky, rustic dish with a dash of Dijon.

¼ cup plus 2 tablespoons butter or margarine, divided
¼ cup all-purpose flour
2 cups half-and-half
1 tablespoon Dijon mustard
¾ teaspoon salt
¼ teaspoon pepper
1½ cups thinly sliced leeks
½ cup chopped sweet red pepper
5 cups thinly sliced new potatoes
2 cups (8 ounces) shredded sharp Cheddar cheese
Garnish: sweet red pepper strips

• **Melt** ¼ cup butter in a heavy saucepan over low heat; add flour, stirring until smooth. Cook, stirring constantly, 1 minute. Gradually stir in half-and-half, and cook over medium heat, stirring constantly, until thickened and bubbly. Stir in mustard, salt, and pepper. Remove pan from heat.

• **Melt** remaining 2 tablespoons butter in a large skillet; add leeks and chopped red pepper. Cook, stirring constantly, until tender.

• **Spoon** ½ cup sauce mixture into a lightly greased 11" x 7" x 1½" baking dish. Layer with half each of potato slices, leek mixture, sauce, and Cheddar cheese. Repeat layers.

• **Cover** and bake at 350° for 50 minutes. Uncover and bake 25 more minutes or until potato slices are tender. Let stand 10 minutes before serving. Garnish, if desired. **Yield:** 8 servings.

Scalloped New Potatoes and Leeks

Cornbread Dressing
Croquettes

Fruited Curry
Rice Bake

CORNBREAD DRESSING CROQUETTES

Give turkey's traditional accompaniment new interest by shaping the dressing into patties and frying them.

2   (6-ounce) packages cornbread mix
3   tablespoons butter or margarine
1   cup chopped celery
1   cup chopped onion
½   cup frozen whole kernel corn, thawed
1   (10¾-ounce) can cream of chicken soup, undiluted
¾   cup milk
¾   cup chicken broth
2   teaspoons rubbed sage
½   teaspoon salt
¼   teaspoon pepper
½   cup yellow cornmeal
½   cup all-purpose flour
Vegetable oil
Garnish: celery leaves

• **Prepare** cornbread according to package directions; cool. Crumble into a large bowl. Melt butter in a large skillet over medium-high heat; add celery, onion, and corn. Cook, stirring constantly, until tender. Stir vegetables, soup, and next 5 ingredients into crumbled cornbread.
• **For** each croquette, shape ½ cup cornbread mixture into a thick patty. Combine cornmeal and flour; roll croquettes in flour mixture. Pour oil to depth of ¼" into a large heavy skillet. Fry croquettes in hot oil over medium-high heat until golden, turning once. Drain on paper towels. Serve warm. Garnish, if desired. **Yield:** 16 croquettes.

FRUITED CURRY RICE BAKE

This dish will fill your kitchen with the rich aromas of curry and cinnamon while it cooks.

1   (8.25-ounce) can pear halves in juice
1   (8-ounce) can pineapple tidbits in juice
¼   cup dried apricots, chopped
¼   cup raisins
3   tablespoons brown sugar
1   teaspoon grated orange rind
2   (14½-ounce) cans ready-to-serve chicken broth
2   cups converted rice, uncooked
¾   teaspoon curry powder
½   teaspoon salt
⅛   teaspoon ground cinnamon
½   cup sliced almonds, toasted

• **Drain** pear and pineapple, reserving juices; chop pear halves. Combine chopped pear, pineapple, apricot, and next 3 ingredients in a large bowl; toss.
• **Add** enough broth to reserved juices to measure 4 cups. Add broth mixture, rice, and next 3 ingredients to fruit mixture; stir well. Pour into a lightly greased 13" x 9" x 2" baking dish.
• **Cover** and bake at 350° for 1 hour or until liquid is absorbed and rice is tender. Let stand 5 minutes before serving. Sprinkle with almonds, and serve immediately. **Yield:** 8 servings.

WALDORF RICE SALAD

An easy mayonnaise-sour cream dressing binds this pretty, fruit-studded salad.

2   oranges, peeled, sectioned, and chopped
1   Red Delicious apple, unpeeled and chopped
1   ripe pear, unpeeled and chopped
2   cups cooked long-grain brown and wild rice blend*
½   cup chopped celery
⅓   cup dried sweetened cranberries* or raisins
½   cup mayonnaise
¼   cup sour cream
Red leaf lettuce leaves (optional)
½   cup chopped walnuts, toasted

• **Combine** first 6 ingredients in a large bowl. Combine mayonnaise and sour cream; add to fruit mixture, tossing well. Cover and chill.

• **Spoon** salad mixture onto individual lettuce-lined salad plates or into a lettuce-lined bowl, if desired. Sprinkle with walnuts just before serving. **Yield:** 8 servings.

*For long-grain brown and wild rice blend, we used Uncle Ben's Rice Trio. For dried sweetened cranberries, we used Ocean Spray Craisins.

Waldorf Rice Salad

CRAN-RASPBERRY CONSERVE

Cook fruit, sugar, and nuts into a thick condiment—a special treat with our scones on the previous page.

4   cups fresh cranberries
¾   cup sugar
½   teaspoon ground cinnamon
¾   cup chopped pecans, toasted
2   tablespoons orange juice
1   (12-ounce) jar red raspberry preserves

• **Combine** first 3 ingredients in a lightly greased 8" baking dish. Cover and bake at 350° for 40 minutes. Remove from oven; stir in pecans, orange juice, and preserves; stir well. Cool. Serve at room temperature or chilled. Store, covered, in refrigerator. **Yield:** 3¾ cups.

CRANBERRIES JUBILEE

Dramatic flambé (flaming) desserts work best when you're hosting a small group of friends. Have your ice cream ready when you strike the match.

1½   cups sugar
1   teaspoon grated orange rind
1   cup freshly squeezed orange juice
4   cups fresh cranberries
3   tablespoons water
1   tablespoon cornstarch
¼   cup brandy
Vanilla ice cream

• **Combine** first 3 ingredients in a large nonstick skillet; bring to a boil, stirring constantly. Reduce heat; add

Cranberry-Pecan Dressing

cranberries, and simmer, uncovered, 3 minutes, stirring mixture occasionally.

• **Combine** water and cornstarch, stirring until smooth; gradually add to cranberry mixture, stirring constantly. Bring to a boil; cook, stirring constantly, 1 minute. Transfer cranberry sauce to a chafing dish or flambé pan; keep warm.

• **Place** brandy in a small, long-handled saucepan; heat until warm (do not boil). Remove from heat. Ignite with a long match; pour over cranberries. Allow flames to die down. Stir well, and serve immediately over ice cream. **Yield:** 8 servings.

CRANBERRY-PECAN DRESSING

Cranberries and pecans add zing to this cornbread dressing.

½   cup butter or margarine
1   cup diced celery
1   cup diced onion
1   clove garlic, chopped
5   cups coarsely crumbled cornbread
4   cups white bread cubes, toasted
2¾ cups chicken broth
1½ cups fresh cranberries
1½ cups chopped pecans, toasted
1   teaspoon grated orange rind
½   cup orange juice
1   tablespoon sugar
½   teaspoon ground cinnamon
¼   teaspoon ground nutmeg
3   large eggs, lightly beaten

• **Melt** butter in a Dutch oven over medium heat. Add celery, onion, and garlic. Cook 10 minutes or until vegetables are tender, stirring occasionally.

• **Stir** cornbread and remaining ingredients into vegetable mixture; spoon mixture into a lightly greased 13" x 9" x 2" baking dish. Bake, uncovered, at 350° for 45 minutes or until lightly browned. **Yield:** 12 servings.

CRANBERRY-MINT SORBET

A light, refreshing touch after a rich, heavy meal. Easy, too, since it's make ahead.

4½ cups water, divided
1¼ cups sugar, divided
¾   cup freshly squeezed orange juice
2   tablespoons chopped fresh mint
2   tablespoons freshly squeezed lemon juice
2¼ cups fresh cranberries
Garnish: fresh mint sprigs

• **Combine** 3¾ cups water and ¾ cup sugar in a large saucepan. Bring to a boil; cook, stirring constantly, until sugar dissolves. Remove from heat; stir in orange juice, chopped mint, and lemon juice. Cool completely.

• **Combine** remaining ¾ cup water, remaining ½ cup sugar, and cranberries in a saucepan; bring to a boil. Cover, reduce heat, and simmer 6 to 8 minutes or until cranberry skins pop. Remove from heat; cool completely.

• **Position** knife blade in food processor bowl; add half of cranberry mixture. Process until smooth, stopping once to scrape down sides. Pour cranberry mixture through a wire-mesh strainer into a bowl, discarding pulp. Repeat procedure with remaining cranberry mixture.

• **Pour** orange juice mixture through a cheesecloth-lined wire-mesh strainer into a bowl, discarding mint. Combine cranberry mixture and orange juice mixture; pour into a 13" x 9" x 2" pan. Cover and freeze until firm.

• **Break** frozen cranberry mixture into large chunks. Position knife blade in food processor bowl; add half of frozen mixture, and process until smooth. Return pureed mixture to pan. Repeat procedure with remaining frozen cranberry mixture. Cover and freeze until firm.

• **Scoop** sorbet into individual serving dishes; garnish, if desired. **Yield:** 7 cups.

SUPPERS
TO SOIREES

ENTERTAINING WITH EASE

One of the season's best gifts is a relaxed gathering of friends
and good food. With our hassle-free recipes and decorating ideas,
you'll enjoy the occasion as much as your guests.

SPARKLY NAPKIN TIES

Cinch your dinner napkins in shiny gold cording
festooned with glittery stars, beads, and balls.

For 6 napkin ties:
9 yards ¼"-diameter cording
low-temperature glue gun and glue sticks
plastic novelty Christmas garland
assorted small Christmas ornaments and beads

1. To make the napkin ties, cut the cording into 6 (54")
pieces. Make tight knots in the ends of each piece. Trim
the raw ends of the cording close to the knots, and apply
a small amount of glue to the ends.
2. To embellish the ties, cut apart the garland into its
individual components. Glue small clusters of the garland
trinkets, ornaments, or beads over the knots in the cording. To add interest, make the clusters slightly different
on each end of the cord. (For example, attach larger ornaments on 1 end and smaller ones on the other.)
3. To wrap the tie around a napkin, fold 1 length of deco-
rated cording in half. Loosely knot the doubled cording
around a napkin.

RIBBON-TRIMMED WOODEN PLATE

Make a set to use as chargers with holiday plates for
your Christmas dinner table.

To trim the plate, on the outside rim of a wooden plate,
measure and mark the spots where you want holes. For the
11" plate pictured here, we drilled holes at ½" and 2¼"
intervals (see diagram below).

Using a drill and a ⅜" drill bit, make holes at the marks.
Thread ribbon through the holes. Tie the ends in a bow on
top of the plate, or knot the ends under the rim.

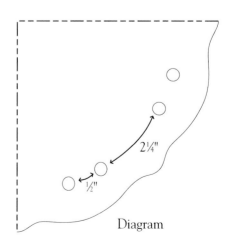

Diagram

RIBBONED TABLE RUNNER

A swath of felt trimmed with ribbons warms a dining room table or sideboard.

diagrams on page 148
½ yard 72"-wide red felt
⅜ yard 72"-wide green felt
7 yards 2"-wide wire-edged ribbon

1. To cut out the table runner, cut the red felt into a 14" x 72" strip. Cut the green felt into a 12" x 70" strip.
2. To cut the point on the end of the red felt, find the midpoint of 1 short side; measure up 5" on 1 long side, and draw a cutting line from this 5" mark to the midpoint of the short side. Repeat for the other long side. Cut along these cutting lines. Repeat for the other end of the red felt. (See Diagram 1.)
3. To cut the point on the end of the green felt, find the midpoint of 1 short side; measure up 4½" on 1 long side, and draw a cutting line from this 4½" mark to the midpoint of the short side. Repeat for the other long side. Cut along these cutting lines. Repeat for the other end of the green felt. (See Diagram 2.)
4. To assemble the table runner, center the green felt over the red felt (green edges should be 1" from red edges). Using pins, mark the slits for the ribbon along each side, beginning 1" in from the 4 corners of the green felt. To mark the ends of the slits, measure 2¼" in toward the center of the runner. (Do not remove pins until the ribbon has been threaded through the slits.) Mark a total of 12 slits along each long edge of the table runner, placing the slits 5⅜" apart. (See Diagram 3.) Cut the slits.
5. To make slits at the points, measure in 1" from the point. Cut 2 (2¼"-long) slits, ¼" on either side of the center of the runner. (See Diagram 3.)
6. To add the ribbon, cut 2 (3½-yard) lengths of ribbon. Weave each ribbon through the slits on the long sides. The ribbon should begin and end from underneath the runner. Center the ribbon so that an equal amount extends from each end of the runner. Bend the ribbon underneath, angling it toward the slits at the point. Pull the ribbon up through these slits and tie the ends in a bow. Trim the raw edges.

HOLIDAY CHAIR SWAG

Bright ribbons and evergreen branches are traditional holiday fare.

For the chair swag, cut a 16" length of 2"-wide wire-edged ribbon, fold the ends to the middle, overlapping slightly, and wire the ribbon loop together at the center to form a small bow. Set aside.

Cut 2 (2-yard) lengths of 2½"-wide ribbon. (To give the bow texture and shape, use 1 length of wire-edged ribbon and 1 length of unwired ribbon.) Lay 1 length of ribbon on top of the other. Treating the 2 layers as one, measure 6" from the end of the ribbon. Pinch the ribbon together, forming the center of the bow. Make a 6" loop and pinch the ribbon again at the center. Twist the ribbon a half-turn and make a 6" loop on the opposite side. Make 1 more loop on each side of the center in the same manner. Twist wire around the center of the bow to secure the ribbon. Fluff the bow by pulling firmly on the loops.

Cut several lengths of 2½"-wide ribbon and metallic cording, and place them behind the large bow to form streamers. Place the small bow in front of the large bow. Using a length of ribbon, tie all of the elements together at the center of the bow. Knot the ribbon at the back to secure. Trim the ribbon ends at an angle for a neat finish. Wire together several branches of evergreen, and tie the evergreen bundle to the back of the bow. Tie small ornaments to the ends of the cording, if desired.

To attach the swag to the chair, use one of the unwired ribbon streamers to tie the swag to the chair back.

For a tree topper, wire 2 swags together back-to-back (without the evergreen), and place the bow on the top of the tree.

PUNCH UP THE HOLIDAYS

Search the pantry for your prettiest bowls to give these
delicious drinks a most dazzling setting.

FIVE-FRUIT PERCOLATOR PUNCH

This spiced drink will scent your kitchen and warm
your guests.

1 (48-ounce) bottle orange-pineapple-apple juice drink
1 (48-ounce) bottle cranberry-apple juice drink
½ cup lemon juice
½ cup firmly packed brown sugar
20 whole allspice
6 (3") sticks cinnamon
Garnish: small lemon slices, cut in half

• **Combine** first 3 ingredients in a large electric percolator. Combine brown sugar, allspice, and cinnamon sticks
in percolator basket. Perk punch through complete cycle
of percolator.
• **Place** 1 lemon slice in each punch cup, if desired; fill
with hot punch. **Yield:** 3½ quarts.

CHOCOLATE EGGNOG

Here's a no-fuss recipe for jazzing up store-bought
eggnog.

2 quarts refrigerated eggnog
1 (16-ounce) can chocolate syrup
½ cup light rum (optional)
1 cup whipping cream
2 tablespoons powdered sugar
Cocoa (optional)

• **Combine** eggnog, syrup, and, if desired, rum in a punch
bowl, stirring well.
• **Beat** whipping cream at high speed of an electric mixer
until foamy. Add powdered sugar, beating until stiff peaks
form. Dollop whipped cream over punch. Sift cocoa over
whipped cream, if desired. **Yield:** 3 quarts.

RASPBERRY SORBET PUNCH

This pretty, sparkling punch is kid-friendly.

1 (64-ounce) bottle cranberry-raspberry juice drink
1 (2-liter) bottle raspberry ginger ale
1 (12-ounce) can frozen pink lemonade concentrate,
      thawed and undiluted
1 quart raspberry sorbet

• **Combine** first 3 ingredients in a large container, stirring
well. Cover and chill 2 hours. Pour chilled mixture into a
large punch bowl. Scoop sorbet into punch. Stir gently.
Yield: 6½ quarts.

CHAMPAGNE BLUSH PUNCH

Chill this pink punch in a wine bottle encased in an
ice block of berries and greenery.

1 (750-milliliter) bottle white Zinfandel*
Holly leaves and berries or pepperberries
1 quart distilled water
1 (10-ounce) jar maraschino cherries with stems,
      undrained
3 (6-ounce) cans pineapple juice
1 (64-ounce) bottle cranberry-cherry juice drink
1 (12-ounce) can frozen lemonade concentrate, thawed
      and undiluted
2 (750-milliliter) bottles champagne, chilled*

• **For ice cylinder,** pour wine into a pitcher; cover and
chill. Rinse out wine bottle, and remove label, using warm
soapy water. Rinse out a half-gallon juice carton or milk carton; cut off top. Place wine bottle in carton. (Do not cork
or cap bottle, or it may break during freezing.) Tape neck of
bottle to top of carton with masking tape to center and
secure it.

Champagne
Blush Punch

• **Arrange** holly leaves and berries between bottle and carton, using a long wooden skewer or handle of a wooden spoon to position leaves and berries. Add distilled water to ½" below top of carton. Freeze at least 8 hours, repositioning leaves and berries as water starts to freeze.

• **Drain** cherries over a large bowl, reserving juice. Reserve cherries to garnish each serving, if desired. Add pineapple juice, cranberry-cherry juice drink, and lemonade concentrate to cherry juice; stir well, and chill.

• **Remove** carton with wine bottle from freezer. Pour cold water into bottle. Dip carton into a sinkful of cold water. (Ice and bottle may crack if warm water is used.)

Tear carton away from ice cylinder. Empty water from wine bottle.

• **Combine** chilled wine, juice mixture, and champagne. Pour punch through a funnel into bottle, refilling as needed. Place ice cylinder upright in a large bowl of crushed ice to slow the melting; insert bottle filled with punch. To serve, gently slip bottle from frozen cylinder (catch drips with a linen towel). **Yield:** 2¼ gallons.

*For nonalcoholic punch, substitute 3 (25.4-ounce) bottles sparkling white grape juice for wine and champagne.

69

Mint Julep
Slush Punch

MINT JULEP SLUSH PUNCH

Lemon and tea heighten the flavor of this Southern favorite.

7   lemon slices
28   small fresh mint sprigs
1   quart distilled water
2   cups sugar
2   cups tap water
½   cup tightly packed fresh mint sprigs
3   regular-size tea bags
2   cups bourbon
2   (33.8-ounce) bottles lemon-flavored sparkling spring
     water, chilled
1   (12-ounce) can frozen orange juice concentrate,
     thawed and undiluted
1   (.23-ounce) envelope unsweetened lemonade mix
1   (2-liter) bottle ginger ale, chilled

• **For fruited ice cubes,** cut each lemon slice into 4 triangles. Place 1 mint sprig and 1 lemon triangle in each compartment of ice cube trays. Fill trays with distilled water; freeze until firm.

• **Bring** sugar and 2 cups tap water to a boil in a large saucepan, stirring until sugar dissolves. Remove from heat; add ½ cup mint sprigs and tea bags. Cover; steep 30 minutes. Remove and discard mint sprigs and tea bags.

• **Combine** mint-tea syrup, bourbon, and next 3 ingredients in a large freezer container; cover and freeze at least 8 hours.

• **To serve,** let frozen bourbon mixture stand at room temperature 1 hour or until slushy. Pour mixture into a large punch bowl; gently stir in ginger ale. Drop lemon-mint ice cubes into punch. **Yield:** 5½ quarts.

FREEZING FACTS

This punch and punch on previous page call for distilled water to make an ice cylinder and ice cubes because regular tap water freezes cloudy and streaked. If you don't have distilled water, bring cold tap water to a boil; then let it cool completely. Or substitute bottled water. Distilled, bottled, and boiled then cooled water will be clearer than tap water when frozen.

WASSAIL

It's tradition to float baked apples in this classic Christmas drink.

8 lady apples or small Gala apples
8 cups water
2 (12-ounce) cans frozen apple juice concentrate, thawed and undiluted
1 (12-ounce) can frozen orange juice concentrate, thawed and undiluted
1 (11.5-ounce) can apricot nectar
1 (6-ounce) can frozen lemonade concentrate, thawed and undiluted
½ cup firmly packed brown sugar
15 whole cloves
6 (3") sticks cinnamon
3 cups Riesling or other sweet white wine*
Garnish: additional cinnamon sticks

• **Peel** top third of each apple. Place apples in a shallow baking dish; pour water to a depth of ½" into dish around apples. Bake, uncovered, at 350° for 50 minutes or until apples are slightly tender, basting occasionally with water. Remove apples from dish; set aside.

• **Combine** 8 cups water and next 7 ingredients in a Dutch oven. Bring to a boil; reduce heat, and simmer, uncovered, 30 minutes. Remove and discard cloves and 6 cinnamon sticks. Stir in wine.

• **Serve** Wassail in Dutch oven, in a slow cooker on low, or in a heatproof punch bowl. Float baked apples in Wassail. Garnish, if desired. **Yield:** about 3¾ quarts.

*For nonalcoholic Wassail, substitute white grape juice for wine.

Wassail

TOMATO CAGE TREES

Tomato cages transformed into sculptural towers set a holiday mood whether on a dining room sideboard or nestled in a terra-cotta pot beside the front door.

44"-tall garden tomato cage

gold spray paint

gold string

fresh greenery branches

hot-glue gun and glue sticks

votive holders and candles

gold cording

clear twinkle lights (optional)

florist's wire (optional)

assorted plastic gift packages and/or fruit

ribbon

1. To prepare the cage, cover all surfaces with gold spray paint. Let dry. Position the cage upside down so the widest tier is at the bottom. Referring to the photograph and using gold string, tie branches of fresh greenery around each tier of the cage. (We used fresh smilax, which stayed fresh-looking indoors for 3 weeks.)

2. To attach the votive holders, hot-glue the bottoms of the votive holders to the tops of the tomato cage tiers, placing them beside the vertical posts. Let dry. Tie strips of gold cording around the votive holders and posts. (You may use twinkle lights instead of votive holders and candles, if desired. Attach the lights to the tomato cage with florist's wire.)

3. To attach the packages or fruit, hot-glue the bottoms and sides of the pieces to the cage. Let dry.

4. To add the ribbon, knot a length of ribbon around the 4 points at the top of the cage; tie the ribbon into a multi-looped bow. (For bow-making directions, see page 145.) Tie additional lengths of ribbon to the bow, and let them trail down the sides of the tree.

COFFEE VOTIVES

This quick-and-easy project makes a great hostess gift.

4"-square glass candle holder with lipped edge
coffee beans (approximately 1 cup)
hot-glue gun and glue sticks
votive candle
clear cellophane (optional)
ribbon (optional)

Using a hot-glue gun, attach 2 rows of coffee beans to
the top edge of the candle holder. Fill in the gaps between
rows with more beans, if necessary. Pour some of the
coffee beans into the bottom of the holder. Place a votive
candle on top of the beans so that the candlewick is
positioned just above the top of the holder. Fill in around
the top and sides of the candle with beans.

Wrap the coffee votives with clear cellophane, and tie
the cellophane with a ribbon, if desired.

NAPKIN TREES

These wire forms make paper napkins an eye-catching table decoration.

plastic-coated clothesline wire
6" Styrofoam cone (for shaping trees)
1" jingle bells
low-temperature glue gun and glue sticks (optional)

1. For each napkin tree, cut a 5' length of wire. To facilitate making the tree shape, wrap the wire smoothly around a rolling pin, creating a tight springlike shape. Beginning at the top of the Styrofoam cone, rewrap the coiled wire onto the cone to form a tree shape. Remove the wire tree from the cone. Adjust the coils to achieve the desired shape.

2. To add the bell, using pliers, turn up approximately 1" of wire at the top of the tree. Slip a jingle bell over the end of the wire. Trim any excess wire above the bell. Secure the bell with a dot of glue, if desired.

3. To use the napkin tree, roll a paper napkin into a cone shape, and place it, pointed end up, inside the wire tree.

Warm Blue Cheese Spread
With Pecans

HOLIDAY HORS D'OEUVRES

Christmas is a time for splurging a little, for piling on pleasures like cheese, nuts, and chocolate. And creating delicious appetizers doesn't have to be hard. Here are some surprisingly quick recipes that don't skimp on flavor.

WARM BLUE CHEESE SPREAD WITH PECANS

A bite of apple, blue cheese, and pecans tastes great in this simple starter.

1   cup chopped pecans
2   tablespoons butter or margarine, melted
2   (8-ounce) packages cream cheese, softened
2   (4-ounce) packages blue cheese
1   cup soft, fresh breadcrumbs
¼   cup chopped fresh parsley
1   tablespoon butter or margarine, melted

• **Toast** pecans in 2 tablespoons butter in a skillet over medium heat, stirring constantly. Remove pecans from heat; cool.
• **Position** knife blade in food processor bowl; add cheeses. Process until smooth, stopping once to scrape down sides. Stir in pecans. Spoon mixture into a greased 1½-quart baking dish.
• **Combine** breadcrumbs, parsley, and 1 tablespoon melted butter; sprinkle crumb mixture over cheese mixture. Bake, uncovered, at 350° for 20 minutes. Serve warm with melba rounds and apple slices. **Yield:** 4 cups.

SPICY VEGGIE-CHEESE SPREAD

Serve this thick spread as a dip, or make it a topping for party sandwiches. Spread it on small rounds of wheat and white bread, and top with cucumber slices.

1   (8-ounce) container garden vegetable process cream
        cheese spread
1   (5-ounce) jar refrigerated pimiento cheese spread
¼   cup mayonnaise
1   teaspoon hot sauce

BAGUETTE TOASTS

Use these dippers for just about any recipe in this chapter. Make them ahead, and store up to two days in an airtight container.

1   baguette
¼   cup olive oil

• **Cut** baguette diagonally into 24 slices (about ½" thick). Brush or drizzle both sides of slices with oil. Place slices close together on a large ungreased baking sheet. Bake at 400° for 4 minutes. Remove from oven; turn slices. Bake 3 to 4 more minutes or until toasted. **Yield:** 2 dozen.

Brush baguette slices with oil, and bake until toasted.

• **Combine** all ingredients in a bowl; stir well. Cover and chill, if desired. Serve with crackers, chips, or assorted raw vegetables. **Yield:** 1½ cups.

PESTO-BRIE TORTA

These creamy baked Brie rounds ooze a heady mix of basil, sun-dried tomatoes, pine nuts, and garlic.

2   (8-ounce) rounds Brie
½   cup chopped fresh basil leaves
½   cup oil-packed sun-dried tomatoes, chopped
½   cup pine nuts
2   cloves garlic, minced
Garnish: fresh basil leaves

• **Remove** rind from top of each Brie, cutting to within ½" of outside edges. Using a sharp knife, slice each Brie in two, making the top slightly thicker than the bottom.
• **Combine** chopped basil, tomato with 2 tablespoons oil from tomato jar, pine nuts, and garlic; stir well.
• **Place** bottom rounds of Brie on an ungreased baking sheet. Spoon ⅓ cup tomato mixture over each round. Top with remaining rounds of Brie, pressing gently. Spoon remaining tomato mixture over each Brie stack; press gently.
• **Bake** at 325° for 10 to 12 minutes or just until Brie is softened but not melted. Serve warm with Baguette Toasts (page 77) or melba rounds. Garnish, if desired. **Yield:** 2 tortas.

Slice each round of Brie in two, making the top half slightly thicker than the bottom.

Pesto-Brie Torta

Walnut-Olive
Marinated Cheese

WALNUT-OLIVE MARINATED CHEESE

Layer goat cheese with roasted olives and walnuts in little jars just meant for gift giving.

1   (4-ounce) log goat cheese or fresh mozzarella
        cheese
¾   teaspoon coarsely ground pepper
¾   cup light olive oil, divided
½   cup pimiento-stuffed olives
½   cup chopped walnuts

• **Carefully** slice cheese into 6 slices; sprinkle cheese slices with pepper, and set aside.

• **Combine** 1 tablespoon oil, olives, and walnuts, tossing to coat. Place on an ungreased jellyroll pan or baking sheet. Bake at 400° for 10 to 13 minutes or until lightly browned. Let mixture cool to touch; coarsely chop.

• **Layer** cheese slices and olive mixture alternately in two 4-ounce jars or one 8-ounce jar. Fill jars with remaining oil. Cover tightly, and keep refrigerated. Serve with Baguette Toasts (page 77) or assorted crackers. **Yield:** 6 appetizer servings.

Note: You can prepare Walnut-Olive Marinated Cheese up to 1 week ahead.

FIG PRESERVES AND ROSEMARY CHEESE

Here's an update of pepper jelly and cream cheese. The flavors of figs, goat cheese, and rosemary unite on a crispy baguette.

1   (8-ounce) package cream cheese, softened
1   (3-ounce) log goat cheese, softened
1   tablespoon chopped fresh rosemary
2   teaspoons honey
1   teaspoon coarsely ground pepper
Fig preserves
Garnish: fresh rosemary sprigs

• **Grease** a miniature loafpan or a 1½-cup mold; line with plastic wrap, making it smooth and allowing edges to extend slightly over edges of pan or mold. Set aside.
• **Position** knife blade in food processor bowl; add first 5 ingredients to bowl. Process 15 seconds or until smooth. (Or beat ingredients at medium speed of an electric mixer until smooth.)
• **Spoon** cheese mixture into prepared pan or mold. Cover and chill at least 2 hours.
• **Unmold** cheese onto a serving plate; remove plastic wrap. Stir preserves, and spoon desired amount over cheese. Garnish, if desired. Serve with Baguette Toasts (page 77), bagel chips, or crackers. **Yield:** 1½ cups.

Note: Don't have the pan or mold for this cheese? Just shape it freeform into a log about 7" or 8" long; wrap it in wax paper to chill. Then unwrap cheese, and spoon preserves over log.

CHEDDAR DATES

Even if you don't like dates, you'll find these addicting. Toasted pecans hide inside dates baked in balls of Cheddar pastry.

1½ cups (6 ounces) shredded sharp Cheddar cheese
1   cup all-purpose flour
1   teaspoon salt
2   teaspoons chopped fresh rosemary
⅓   cup butter or margarine, melted
24 pitted dates
24 pecan halves, toasted
1   egg white, lightly beaten
¼   teaspoon sugar

• **Combine** first 4 ingredients, stirring well. Add butter, stirring just until dry ingredients are moistened. (Dough will be crumbly.)
• **Make** a lengthwise slit in each date, and stuff each with a pecan half. Press 1 generous tablespoon cheese mixture around each date, covering completely. Cover and chill 45 minutes. (You can cover and freeze dates up to 1 month.)
• **Place** dates on a greased baking sheet, and brush with egg white. Sprinkle with sugar. Bake at 350° for 25 minutes. Remove dates to a wire rack to cool. Serve warm or at room temperature. **Yield:** 2 dozen.

Make a lengthwise slit in each pitted date, and insert a pecan half.

Press 1 generous tablespoon cheese dough around each date, covering completely.

Cheddar
Dates

Fig Preserves and
Rosemary Cheese

WINE AND CHEESE MINI MUFFINS

Serve these on a silver tray with grapes, cheese, and apple and pear slices. And wine, of course.

2   cups all-purpose flour
1   tablespoon baking powder
¼   teaspoon salt
1   cup (4 ounces) shredded Swiss cheese
⅓   cup grated Parmigiano-Reggiano cheese
¾   teaspoon dried oregano or thyme
2   egg yolks, lightly beaten
½   cup milk
½   cup dry white wine
2   tablespoons vegetable oil
Vegetable cooking spray

• **Combine** first 6 ingredients in a large bowl; make a well in center of mixture. Combine egg yolks and next 3 ingredients; add to dry ingredients, stirring just until moistened. Spoon batter into miniature (1¾") muffin pans coated with cooking spray, filling two-thirds full.
• **Bake** at 375° for 20 to 22 minutes. Remove from pans immediately. Serve warm. **Yield:** 3 dozen.

HERBED CHICKEN PIZZAS

An easy, filling snack when the occasion calls for substantial hors d'oeuvres.

2   (3-ounce) packages cream cheese, softened
¼   cup fines herbes soup mix*
2   tablespoons white vinegar or white balsamic vinegar
1   clove garlic, crushed
2   (8-ounce) packages Italian pizza crusts*
½   cup sun-dried tomatoes packed in oil, drained and
        thinly sliced
1   deli-roasted chicken breast, finely shredded
        (about 2 cups)
1½   cups (6 ounces) shredded mozzarella cheese

• **Position** knife blade in food processor bowl; add first 4 ingredients. Process until smooth, stopping once to scrape

down sides (or beat first 4 ingredients at medium speed of an electric mixer until smooth).
• **Spread** mixture evenly over pizza crusts. Sprinkle with tomato, chicken, and mozzarella. Place pizzas on a baking sheet. Bake at 400° for 10 minutes or until cheese melts. Cut each pizza into 6 wedges. **Yield:** 24 appetizer servings.

*For soup mix, we used Knorr. For pizza crusts, we used Boboli; two individual crusts come in each 8-ounce package.

PIZZA FONDUE AND BISCOTTI

Fondue's back, and this version earned our staff's highest rating. The savory make-ahead biscotti are flecked with sun-dried tomato bits.

2   (11-ounce) cans fiesta nacho cheese soup, undiluted
1½   cups (6 ounces) shredded Monterey Jack cheese or
        4-cheese blend
¾   cup pizza sauce
½   cup milk
1   teaspoon dried Italian seasoning
½   cup chopped pepperoni
Pizza Biscotti (optional)

• **Combine** first 5 ingredients in a heavy saucepan; cook over medium heat, stirring constantly, until cheese melts and mixture is smooth. Stir in pepperoni. Spoon mixture into a fondue pot or chafing dish. Serve with Pizza Biscotti, if desired, or your favorite chips. **Yield:** 4 cups.

PIZZA BISCOTTI

3   cups all-purpose flour
1   teaspoon baking powder
1   teaspoon kosher (coarse) salt
½   cup oil-packed sun-dried tomatoes, drained and
        finely chopped
2   teaspoons dried oregano
½   teaspoon coarsely ground pepper
3   large eggs
½   cup water
2   tablespoons olive oil

Pizza Fondue
and Biscotti

• **Combine** first 6 ingredients in a large bowl, stirring well. Combine 2 eggs, water, and oil, stirring well. Add to dry ingredients, stirring just until dry ingredients are moistened.

• **Turn** dough out onto a lightly floured surface; divide dough in half. Shape each half into a 2½"-wide log. Place logs on a greased baking sheet. Beat remaining egg, and brush over logs.

• **Bake** at 350° for 35 minutes. Cool to touch. Working very carefully with a sharp knife, cut logs diagonally into ¼" slices.

• **Bake** slices at 350° for 20 to 22 more minutes. Transfer biscotti to a wire rack; cool completely. Store in an air-tight container up to 2 weeks. **Yield:** 2 dozen.

Orange
Pomanders

FAST & FESTIVE CENTERPIECES

Brighten tables and sideboards with these inexpensive centerpieces
you can assemble with ease before guests arrive.

ORANGE POMANDERS

At first glance, these oranges appear studded with pearls, making for a dressy, festive look.

Stick corsage pins in oranges and stack the oranges on an elegant pedestal or in a sparkling glass bowl. Fill in and soften gaps with short lengths of wire-edged ribbon folded in half and twisted into loops. Lemons or limes are a suitable substitute for oranges, or you can use a combination of all three. Packages of corsage pins are available at craft and discount stores.

BRUSSELS SPROUTS & CRANBERRY TREE

Guests will love the surprise of brussels sprouts in this imaginative, fun centerpiece.

Use wooden toothpicks to attach fresh brussels sprouts to a 12" Styrofoam cone. Using the same technique, tuck cranberries among the brussels sprouts to fill in gaps and add a festive touch of color to the centerpiece.

SUGARED FRUIT

Dainty fruit rolled in sugar—always appealing—is a classic Christmas trimming.

Brush clean, dry fruit with egg whites; then roll the fruit in sugar. Place the sugared fruit on wire racks to dry. For the centerpiece, stack the fruit in a clear glass container. Drop in a few unsugared cranberries, if desired. (This is a quick centerpiece to assemble; however, you may want to sugar-coat the fruit the night before to give the coating plenty of time to dry.)

Brussels Sprouts & Cranberry Tree

Sugared Fruit

FIRESIDE SUPPER

Create a cozy setting before a crackling fire with a garland on the mantel and soothing jazz in the background.

Serves 6 to 8

Spiced Red Zinger Cider

Shrimp and Sausage Gumbo with
Winter Greens

Mixed Greens with Hot Bacon-Honey
Mustard Dressing

Cornmeal Focaccia

White Chocolate-Almond Blondies

Coffee

MAKE-AHEAD PLAN

TWO OR THREE DAYS AHEAD:
- Make cider and salad dressing; chill.

ONE DAY AHEAD:
- Prepare gumbo, but don't add shrimp. Cover and chill.
- Peel shrimp, and, if desired, devein. Cover and chill.
- Prepare rice for gumbo. Cover and chill.
- Wash salad greens. Place greens in zip-top plastic bag with damp paper towels. Chill.
- Bake brownies. Store in an airtight container.

THE MORNING OF:
- Bake focaccia. Let cool, and cover with aluminum foil.

20 TO 30 MINUTES AHEAD:
- Reheat gumbo; add shrimp, and cook as directed.
- Reheat cider and dressing.
- Reheat rice in microwave.
- Reheat focaccia in foil at 350°.

SPICED RED ZINGER CIDER

Serve flavored, toasted nuts for guests to munch while they sip this zesty cider.

1   quart water
6   Red Zinger tea bags
24   whole cloves
1   orange
Cheesecloth
24   whole allspice
3   (3") sticks cinnamon, broken
5   cups apple cider
5   cups cranberry juice drink
½   cup sugar
1½ to 2 cups dark rum*
Garnish: additional 3" sticks cinnamon

• **Bring** water to a boil; add tea bags. Remove from heat; cover and steep 5 minutes. Remove and discard tea bags.
• **Insert** cloves into skin of orange. Cut a 6" square of cheesecloth; place allspice and broken cinnamon sticks in center, and tie with string.
• **Combine** tea, orange, spice bag, cider, cranberry juice, and sugar in a Dutch oven; bring to a boil. Cover, reduce heat, and simmer 1 hour. Remove from heat; cool to room temperature. Remove and discard orange and spice

bag. (At this point, you can refrigerate mixture in a non-metal airtight container up to 3 days.)
• **To serve,** combine cider mixture and rum in Dutch oven; cook over low heat until hot, stirring occasionally. Ladle cider into mugs; serve warm with cinnamon-stick stirrers, if desired. **Yield:** 14 cups.

*For dark rum, we used Myers. It comes from Jamaica and costs a little more, but it's worth it for such smooth flavor.

SHRIMP AND SAUSAGE GUMBO WITH WINTER GREENS

Good-luck greens add a healthy note to this rich gumbo.

1   (16-ounce) package andouille sausage or other
        smoked sausage, cut into ½" slices
2   cups chopped onion
1½   cups chopped sweet red pepper
2   large cloves garlic, minced
½   cup plus 2 tablespoons vegetable oil, divided
½   cup all-purpose flour
2   (14½-ounce) cans chicken broth
2   (14½-ounce) cans diced tomatoes, undrained
¾   pound washed and trimmed turnip greens or other
        greens
1   tablespoon dried thyme
1   teaspoon salt
1   teaspoon freshly ground pepper
1   teaspoon hot sauce
2   bay leaves
1   pound unpeeled medium-size fresh shrimp
Gumbo filé (optional)
Hot cooked rice

• **Cook** first 4 ingredients in 2 tablespoons hot oil in a Dutch oven over medium-high heat, stirring constantly, until sausage is browned and vegetables are tender. Remove sausage and vegetables from Dutch oven; drain and set aside.
• **Combine** remaining ½ cup oil and flour in Dutch oven; cook over medium heat, stirring constantly, until

Spiced Red Zinger Cider

Shrimp and Sausage Gumbo
with Winter Greens

Mixed Greens with Hot
Bacon-Honey Mustard
Dressing

Cornmeal
Focaccia

roux is chocolate-colored (20 to 25 minutes). Gradually add broth, stirring constantly.

• **Add** sausage mixture, tomatoes, and next 6 ingredients; bring to a boil. Cover, reduce heat, and simmer 30 minutes, stirring occasionally. Uncover and simmer 25 more minutes, stirring occasionally.

• **Peel** shrimp, and devein, if desired. Add shrimp to gumbo; cook 5 minutes or until shrimp turn pink, stirring occasionally. Remove from heat; remove and discard bay leaves. Add gumbo filé, if desired. Serve gumbo over hot cooked rice. **Yield:** 3 quarts.

MIXED GREENS WITH HOT BACON-HONEY MUSTARD DRESSING

This high-flavor salad (pictured on page 91) is a highlight in this filling meal.

8   slices bacon
3   tablespoon sherry vinegar
3   tablespoons vegetable oil
1½   tablespoons prepared mustard
1½   tablespoons honey
12   cups loosely packed torn mixed salad greens or baby lettuces
¾   cup crumbled blue cheese

• **Cook** bacon in a large skillet over medium heat until crisp; remove bacon, reserving 3 tablespoons drippings in skillet. Crumble bacon, and set aside.

• **Add** vinegar and next 3 ingredients to drippings in skillet. Bring to a boil over medium-high heat, stirring constantly with a wire whisk. Remove from heat.

• **Place** mixed greens in a salad bowl. Pour hot dressing over greens, and toss gently. Sprinkle with crumbled bacon and blue cheese. Serve immediately. **Yield:** 6 to 8 servings.

CORNMEAL FOCACCIA

This European flatbread (pictured on page 91) gets the Southern treatment with the addition of cornmeal.

½   cup olive oil, divided
¾   cup minced onion
2   cloves garlic, minced
1½   cups warm water (105° to 115°)
2   teaspoons salt
2   packages active dry yeast
2   cups cornmeal
3¾   cups all-purpose flour, divided
2   teaspoons kosher (coarse) salt

• **Heat** ¼ cup olive oil in a skillet over medium heat; add onion and garlic. Cook, stirring constantly, 5 minutes.

Transfer mixture to a large bowl. Add water, 2 teaspoons salt, and yeast; stir well.

• **Add** cornmeal and 2 cups flour; stir just until dry ingredients are moistened. Gradually stir in enough remaining flour to make a soft dough.

• **Turn** dough out onto a floured surface; knead until smooth and elastic (about 5 minutes). Place dough in a bowl coated with olive oil, turning to grease top. Cover and let rise in a warm place (85°), free from drafts, 1 hour or until doubled in bulk.

• **Coat** a 15" x 10" x 1" jellyroll pan with olive oil. Turn dough out into pan. Press dough to edges of pan. Cover and let rise in a warm place, free from drafts, 30 to 45 minutes or until doubled in bulk.

• **Dimple** the dough at 1" intervals, using the handle of a wooden spoon or fingertips. Coat top of dough with remaining ¼ cup olive oil; sprinkle with kosher salt.

• **Bake** at 425° for 25 to 30 minutes or until golden. Remove from pan, and serve immediately; or cool on wire racks, and serve at room temperature. **Yield:** 6 to 8 servings.

WHITE CHOCOLATE-ALMOND BLONDIES

These chewy blonde brownies are full of almonds and buttery white chocolate bits.

2   cups all-purpose flour
1½   teaspoons baking powder
½   teaspoon salt
⅔   cup butter or margarine
1½   teaspoons instant coffee granules
2   cups firmly packed brown sugar
2   large eggs, lightly beaten
1   cup whole natural almonds, coarsely chopped and toasted
1   cup (6 ounces) white chocolate morsels

• **Combine** flour, baking powder, and salt in a bowl; set aside.

• **Melt** butter in a large saucepan over medium-low heat. Add coffee granules, stirring until dissolved. Remove

White Chocolate-
Almond Blondies

from heat. Add brown sugar and eggs; stir well. Gradually stir in flour mixture. Add almonds and white chocolate morsels, stirring well.

• **Spread** batter in a lightly greased 13" x 9" x 2" pan. Bake at 350° for 30 minutes. Cool completely in pan on a wire rack. Cut into squares. **Yield:** 2½ dozen.

GIFTS OF
GOOD TASTE

HOLIDAY BREADS

Make these your bread-and-butter gifts for the season: flaky biscuits, luscious coffee cakes, butters infused with fresh herbs. Keep some for yourself to serve when unexpected guests arrive.

Sweet Potato
Biscuits

Sticky Bun
Biscuits

SWEET POTATO BISCUITS

Caraway seeds lend a nutty, delicate anise flavor to these moist biscuits. Tuck slivers of smoked turkey or ham inside, and serve them with whole-berry cranberry sauce on a holiday buffet.

2   cups all-purpose flour
1   tablespoon baking powder
1   tablespoon sugar
½   teaspoon salt
½   teaspoon caraway seeds
1   cup canned mashed sweet potato
¾   cup whipping cream

• **Combine** first 5 ingredients, stirring well. Combine sweet potato and whipping cream; add to dry ingredients, stirring just until dry ingredients are moistened.
• **Turn** dough out onto a lightly floured surface; knead 4 or 5 times. Roll or pat dough to ¾" thickness; cut with a 2" or 2½" biscuit cutter, and place on a lightly greased baking sheet. Bake at 425° for 12 to 15 minutes or until golden. Serve warm. **Yield:** 16 biscuits.

Note: You can also cut out these biscuits using your favorite cookie cutters, such as a 2½" star cutter used for biscuits shown in the top of the photo at left.

STICKY BUN BISCUITS

For the ultimate breakfast, add coffee and fresh fruit.

1   cup firmly packed brown sugar
¾   cup butter or margarine
½   cup light corn syrup
1   cup coarsely chopped pecans
3   cups self-rising flour
¼   cup sugar
¾   cup shortening
1   cup milk

• **Combine** first 3 ingredients in a saucepan; cook over medium heat, stirring constantly, until melted and smooth. Pour mixture into a greased 13" x 9" x 2" pan; sprinkle with pecans. Set aside.
• **Combine** flour and ¼ cup sugar; cut in shortening with a pastry blender until mixture is crumbly. Add milk, stirring until dry ingredients are moistened. Turn dough out onto a lightly floured surface; knead lightly 4 or 5 times.
• **Roll** dough to ¾" thickness; cut with a 2" biscuit cutter. Place biscuits over brown sugar mixture in pan. Bake at 400° for 18 to 20 minutes or until done. Remove from oven, and let stand 5 minutes. Invert onto a serving platter; remove pan. Spoon any additional brown sugar glaze over biscuits; serve immediately. **Yield:** 1½ dozen.

Spicy Pepperoni
Biscuits

LITTLE ROSEMARY AND HONEY BISCUITS

If you don't have miniature muffin pans, drop dough by rounded tablespoonfuls onto ungreased baking sheets; bake at 400° for 10 minutes.

1   cup self-rising flour
1½ tablespoons chopped fresh rosemary
⅓   cup cold butter, cut up
1   (8-ounce) package cream cheese, softened
1½ tablespoons honey

• **Combine** flour and rosemary; cut in butter with a pastry blender until crumbly. Beat cream cheese and honey at medium speed of an electric mixer until creamy. Add flour mixture; beat at low speed just until dry ingredients are moistened. Spoon dough into ungreased miniature (1¾") muffin pans, filling full. Bake at 400° for 14 to 16 minutes or until golden. Serve warm. **Yield:** 20 biscuits.

OATMEAL SKILLET BREAD

Old World scones were made with oats and baked on a griddle. Our version bakes in a skillet with a sprinkling of oats for texture and a pretty top.

2   cups all-purpose flour
½   teaspoon baking soda
¾   teaspoon salt
⅓   cup quick-cooking oats, uncooked and divided
¼   cup cold butter or margarine, cut up
1   large egg, lightly beaten
1   cup buttermilk
2   tablespoons brown sugar

• **Combine** flour, soda, salt, and 3 tablespoons oats in a bowl; cut in butter with a pastry blender until mixture is crumbly. Combine egg, buttermilk, and brown sugar; add to flour mixture, stirring with a fork just until dry ingredients are moistened.
• **Spread** dough in a greased 9" cast-iron skillet. Sprinkle with remaining oats. Bake at 425° for 25 minutes. Cut into wedges; serve warm with preserves. **Yield:** 8 servings.

SPICY PEPPERONI BISCUITS

Serve these warm biscuits for brunch with mugs of cheese soup.

2   cups all-purpose flour
1   tablespoon baking powder
½   teaspoon salt
½   teaspoon dry mustard
¼   teaspoon ground red pepper
⅓   cup shortening
½   cup finely chopped pepperoni*
¾   cup milk

• **Combine** first 5 ingredients; cut in shortening with a pastry blender until mixture is crumbly. Stir in pepperoni. Add milk, stirring just until dry ingredients are moistened.
• **Turn** dough out onto a lightly floured surface; knead 3 or 4 times. Roll dough to ½" thickness; cut dough with a 2" or 2½" biscuit cutter, and place biscuits on a lightly greased baking sheet. Bake at 425° for 13 to 15 minutes or until lightly browned. **Yield:** 1 dozen.

*Sliced pepperoni is easy to chop. Look for a 3.5-ounce package near sandwich meats at the supermarket.

Oatmeal Skillet
Bread

Savory Sausage-
Swiss Muffins

Streusel Cran-
Orange Muffins

SAVORY SAUSAGE-SWISS MUFFINS

Reheat leftover muffins in the microwave; one muffin heats in 20 to 30 seconds at HIGH.

½ pound mild or spicy ground pork sausage
1¾ cups biscuit and baking mix
½ cup (2 ounces) shredded Swiss cheese
¾ teaspoon ground sage
¼ teaspoon dried thyme
1 large egg, lightly beaten
½ cup milk

• **Brown** sausage in a skillet over medium heat, stirring until it crumbles. Drain well. Combine sausage, biscuit mix, and next 3 ingredients in a bowl; make a well in center of mixture.
• **Combine** egg and milk; add to dry ingredients, stirring just until moistened. Spoon batter into greased muffin pans, filling two-thirds full. Bake at 375° for 22 minutes or until golden. Serve warm. Store leftovers in refrigerator. **Yield:** 1 dozen.

STREUSEL CRAN-ORANGE MUFFINS

1½ cups all-purpose flour
1 teaspoon baking powder
½ teaspoon baking soda
½ teaspoon salt
1 large egg, lightly beaten
½ cup cranberry-orange relish
1 teaspoon grated orange rind
⅓ cup freshly squeezed orange juice
¼ cup firmly packed brown sugar
¼ cup butter or margarine, melted
⅓ cup chopped pecans
¼ cup firmly packed brown sugar
½ teaspoon ground cinnamon

• **Combine** first 4 ingredients in a large bowl; make a well in center of mixture. Combine egg and next 5 ingredients; add to dry ingredients, stirring just until moistened. Spoon into greased muffin pans, filling two-thirds full.

• **Combine** pecans, ¼ cup brown sugar, and cinnamon; sprinkle over muffins. Bake at 400° for 15 minutes or until golden. Remove from pans immediately. **Yield:** 1 dozen.

DRIED CHERRY-LEMON COFFEE CAKE

½ cup butter or margarine, softened
¾ cup sugar
2 large eggs
2 cups all-purpose flour
2 teaspoons baking powder
1 teaspoon baking soda
⅛ teaspoon salt
1 tablespoon grated lemon rind
1 cup buttermilk
2 tablespoons freshly squeezed lemon juice
2 (3-ounce) packages dried cherries
½ cup chopped pecans
1 teaspoon vanilla extract
Lemon Glaze

• **Beat** butter at medium speed of an electric mixer until creamy; gradually add sugar, beating well. Add eggs, one at a time, beating well after each addition.
• **Combine** flour and next 4 ingredients. Combine buttermilk and lemon juice. Add flour mixture to butter mixture alternately with buttermilk mixture, beginning and ending with flour mixture. Beat at low speed after each addition until blended. Stir in cherries, pecans, and vanilla. Pour batter into a greased 6-cup Bundt pan.
• **Bake** at 350° for 45 minutes or until a wooden pick inserted in center comes out clean. Cool in pan on a wire rack 10 minutes; remove from pan, and cool completely on wire rack. Drizzle with glaze. **Yield:** one 8" coffee cake.

LEMON GLAZE

½ cup sifted powdered sugar
1 teaspoon grated lemon rind
1 tablespoon freshly squeezed lemon juice

• **Combine** all ingredients, stirring until sugar dissolves. **Yield:** ¼ cup.

CINNAMON-SOUR CREAM STREUSEL LOAF

Sour cream makes this little loaf luscious.

½ cup butter or margarine, softened

1 cup sugar

1 large egg

1¼ cups all-purpose flour

½ teaspoon baking powder

¼ teaspoon salt

½ cup sour cream

½ teaspoon vanilla extract

½ cup chopped pecans

¼ cup firmly packed brown sugar

1 tablespoon sugar

½ teaspoon ground cinnamon

• **Beat** butter at medium speed of an electric mixer until creamy; gradually add 1 cup sugar, beating well. Add egg, beating until blended.

• **Combine** flour, baking powder, and salt; add to butter mixture alternately with sour cream, beginning and ending with flour mixture. Beat at low speed just until blended. Stir in vanilla.

• **Combine** pecans and remaining 3 ingredients. Pour half of batter into a greased and floured 8½" x 4½" x 3" loaf-pan; sprinkle with half of pecan mixture. Pour remaining batter into pan; top with remaining pecan mixture.

• **Bake** at 350° for 1 hour or until wooden pick inserted in center comes out clean. (Cover with aluminum foil during last 15 minutes of baking to prevent excessive browning, if necessary.) Cool in pan on a wire rack 10 minutes; remove from pan, and cool completely. **Yield:** 1 loaf.

Cinnamon-Sour
Cream Streusel Loaf

Squash and Onion
Cheese Bread

SQUASH AND ONION CHEESE BREAD

This recipe has its roots in Southern-style squash casserole. Slice the loaf, and toast it with extra cheese for a midmorning or afternoon snack.

½   (16-ounce) package frozen yellow squash, thawed
1   cup chopped onion
3   tablespoons butter or margarine, melted
¼   teaspoon salt
2   cups biscuit and baking mix
¾   cup (3 ounces) shredded sharp Cheddar cheese
½   teaspoon poultry seasoning
¼   teaspoon freshly ground pepper
1   large egg, lightly beaten
⅔   cup milk

• **Squeeze** excess liquid from squash, using several layers of paper towels; coarsely chop squash.
• **Cook** squash and onion in butter in a large skillet over medium-high heat until onion is tender and most of liquid is evaporated; stir in salt. Remove squash mixture from heat, and cool completely.
• **Combine** biscuit mix and next 3 ingredients in a large bowl. Combine egg and milk; add to dry ingredients, stirring just until dry ingredients are moistened. Stir in squash mixture. Spoon batter into a well-greased 8½" x 4½" x 3" loafpan.
• **Bake** at 375° for 50 minutes or until a wooden pick inserted in center comes out clean. Cool in pan on a wire rack 10 minutes. Remove from pan; cool completely on wire rack. **Yield:** 1 loaf.

Note: To wrap bread for gift giving, seal loaf in a gallon-size zip-top plastic bag. Tie Christmas ribbon around wrapped loaf, folding zip-top under loaf.

ORANGE MARMALADE COFFEE CAKE

Sweet marmalade and cream cheese nearly make a dessert of this easy breakfast cake.

1   (8-ounce) package cream cheese, softened
½   cup butter or margarine, softened
¾   cup firmly packed brown sugar
2   large eggs, lightly beaten
¼   cup milk
1   teaspoon vanilla extract
2   cups all-purpose flour
2   teaspoons baking powder
¼   teaspoon salt
1   (18-ounce) jar orange marmalade or other marmalade or preserves
½   cup chopped pecans
¼   cup firmly packed brown sugar
1   tablespoon all-purpose flour
1   tablespoon butter or margarine, melted
¾   cup sifted powdered sugar
1   tablespoon milk

• **Beat** cream cheese and ½ cup butter at medium speed of an electric mixer until creamy; gradually add ¾ cup brown sugar, beating well. Combine eggs, ¼ cup milk, and vanilla; add to cream cheese mixture. Beat well.
• **Combine** 2 cups flour, baking powder, and salt; add to cream cheese mixture, beating at low speed until blended. Spoon half of batter into a greased and floured 13" x 9" x 2" pan. Stir marmalade. Spread marmalade over batter in pan. Dollop remaining batter over marmalade. Combine pecans and next 3 ingredients, stirring well. Sprinkle over batter in pan.
• **Bake** at 350° for 40 minutes or until a wooden pick inserted in center comes out clean. Cool 15 minutes.
• **Combine** powdered sugar and 1 tablespoon milk; stir well. Drizzle over coffee cake. Cut into squares to serve. **Yield:** 15 servings.

CREAM CHEESE BRAIDS

The perfect food for Christmas morning—beautiful braided bread that oozes cream cheese when sliced.

1   (16-ounce) package hot roll mix
1   (8-ounce) package cream cheese, softened
⅓   cup sugar
1   teaspoon vanilla extract
1   egg yolk
Pinch of salt
1   egg yolk, lightly beaten
1   cup sifted powdered sugar
1   tablespoon milk
1   teaspoon vanilla extract

• **Prepare** dough from hot roll mix according to package directions, using yeast packet. Turn dough out onto a lightly floured surface, and knead 4 or 5 times. Divide dough in half. Roll each portion of dough to a 12" x 8" rectangle.

• **Position** knife blade in food processor bowl; add cream cheese and next 4 ingredients to bowl. Process until blended. (Or beat cream cheese and next 4 ingredients at medium speed of an electric mixer until blended.) Spread half of cream cheese mixture lengthwise down center of each dough rectangle.

• **Working** with 1 dough rectangle at a time, cut nine 3" deep slits into each long side of dough. Fold strips over cream cheese filling, alternating sides and making a braid. Pinch ends to seal, and tuck under, if desired. Carefully place loaves on greased baking sheets.

• **Cover** and let rise in a warm place (85°), free from drafts, 30 minutes. Brush tops with beaten egg yolk. Bake at 375° for 15 minutes or until golden.

• **Combine** powdered sugar, milk, and 1 teaspoon vanilla, stirring well; drizzle over warm loaves. **Yield:** two 12" loaves.

Cream Cheese Braid

Cornmeal-Pecan Waffles

CORNMEAL-PECAN WAFFLES

Sifting dry ingredients leads to light-textured waffles. Country Ham and Sage Butter on page 108 makes a distinctive complement.

1   cup all-purpose flour
¾   cup yellow cornmeal
2   teaspoons baking powder
½   teaspoon baking soda
¼   teaspoon salt
3   large eggs, lightly beaten
1½ cups buttermilk
½   cup vegetable oil
1   teaspoon vanilla extract
1   cup chopped pecans, toasted
Vegetable cooking spray or oil
Powdered sugar

• **Sift** first 5 ingredients into a large bowl.
• **Combine** eggs and next 3 ingredients, stirring well. Add to flour mixture, stirring just until blended. Stir in pecans.
• **Coat** a waffle iron with cooking spray or oil; allow iron to preheat. Pour 1 cup batter onto hot waffle iron, quickly spreading batter to edges. Bake until steaming stops and waffles are crisp. Sift powdered sugar over waffles; if desired, serve with Country Ham and Sage Butter (page 108). **Yield:** 16 (4") waffles.

Note: To keep the first batch of waffles warm while baking remaining waffles, transfer them to a baking sheet and place them, uncovered, in a 300° oven up to 5 minutes.

GIFT CANISTERS

Recycle food containers by embellishing them with natural or found materials.
They're great for giving gourmet coffee or dried herbs from your garden.

Wash and dry empty food containers such as potato chip
canisters, coffee, mixed nut, or orange juice cans. Using
hot glue, completely cover the cans with a variety of
materials, including twigs, kraft paper (or brown paper
bags), burlap, twine, or newspaper.

For the newspaper-covered container, use a rubber
stamp to print a design on a piece of newspaper large
enough to cover the can. Let dry. To cover the can, place
it in the center of the piece of newspaper. Gently pull the

newspaper to the top of the can and fold the top edge to
the inside, creasing and flattening the paper as needed.
Use a dot of glue to hold paper on the inside of the can as
needed. Wrap a square piece of newspaper around the lid,
gather the paper at the top, and tie with twine.

To trim the packages, use hot glue to attach pebbles,
nuts, leaves, or ribbons. Cut lengths of twine to form
letters. Hot-glue a Christmas message on the container,
if desired.

110

PLUSH GIFT BAGS

Use a variety of fabrics such as silk, flannel, or classic cotton to wrap gifts in style.

To create a pattern, using a compass, pencil and string, or any flat, round object as a guide, trace a circle of the desired size onto paper and cut it out. The circle size will depend on the size of the gift you want to wrap. (The bags pictured are made from a 20" circle.)

Place the pattern on the fabric of your choice, and cut out the circle. (You will need approximately ½ yard of fabric for 2 bags.) Using pinking shears, trim the raw edge.

To form the casing, with wrong sides facing, turn under 1" around the edges and machine-stitch. Use a pair of scissors to make a small slit in the casing, and thread ribbon or cording through the casing, knotting the ends. Pull both ends of the ribbon to gather the top of the gift bag, and tie in a bow to close.

To trim the fabric bags, tuck silk flowers, cinnamon sticks, or greenery into the opening, if desired.

FESTIVE FRAMES

Friends and family will appreciate these pretty frames for displaying holiday photos—this year and every year after.

Turn an inexpensive purchased frame into a work of art by embellishing it with a combination of silk or dried florals, berries, cinnamon sticks, and ribbons. Experiment with different arrangements by cutting the stems apart and mixing flowers or berries from 1 stem with the foliage from another. Use a low-temperature glue gun to attach materials to the frames.

MAILING BOWS

Afraid that your long-distance gifts will arrive with flattened bows?
These look crisp no matter how far they travel.

patterns on pages 150-151

tracing paper

craft glue

10"-square Christmas wrapping paper (for 10" bow)

10"-square black foam-core board (for 10" bow)

6"-square Christmas wrapping paper (for 6" bow)

6"-square black foam-core board (for 6" bow)

craft knife

black paint pen

double-sided tape

contrasting paper for "tag"

1. To make each bow, trace the bow pattern and cut it

out. Using a thin coat of glue, affix the wrapping paper to the foam-core board, smoothing the wrinkles from the paper. Trace the pattern onto the wrapping-paper side of the foam-core board.

2. To cut out the bow, using a craft knife, carefully cut around the outer edges. Using a paint pen, touch up the edges, if necessary, and outline all the design lines of the bow. Place double-sided tape on the back of the bow, and affix it to the package to be mailed.

3. To make the tag, cut contrasting paper to fit the space on the pattern for the tag. Using a black paint pen, outline all the design lines of the tag. Referring to the photograph, glue the tag on the bow.

COOKIE COMPENDIUM

We've got great recipes to fill your every party tray,
cookie jar, and gift basket.

CHEWY CHOCOLATE-CINNAMON COOKIES

Instant pudding mix makes these cookies soft and
chewy.

1   cup butter, softened
½   cup sugar
½   cup firmly packed brown sugar
1   (3.9-ounce) package chocolate fudge instant
      pudding mix
2   large eggs
2   teaspoons vanilla extract
2¼ cups all-purpose flour
1   teaspoon baking soda
2   teaspoons ground cinnamon
1   (11.5-ounce) package semisweet chocolate mega
      morsels
1   (2½-ounce) package walnut pieces, toasted and
      chopped (⅔ cup)

• **Beat** butter at medium speed of an electric mixer until
creamy; gradually add sugars and pudding mix, beating
well. Add eggs and vanilla; beat well.
• **Combine** flour, soda, and cinnamon; gradually add to
butter mixture, beating just until blended (do not over-
beat). Stir in chocolate morsels and walnuts.
• **Drop** dough by tablespoonfuls onto lightly greased
cookie sheets. Bake at 350° for 9 minutes. Cool on cookie
sheets 1 minute. Remove cookies to wire racks; cool completely. **Yield:** 5 dozen.

*Note: If you don't have a package of mega morsels on hand,
you can use 1 (12-ounce) package regular semisweet chocolate
morsels.*

COFFEE BEAN COOKIES

These drop cookies are studded with chocolate-
covered coffee beans, chunks of toffee candy bars, and
almonds.

½   cup butter, softened
½   cup shortening
¾   cup sugar
¾   cup firmly packed brown sugar
2   large eggs
1   teaspoon vanilla extract
2¼ cups all-purpose flour
1   teaspoon baking soda
1   teaspoon salt
½   teaspoon ground cinnamon
1   cup chopped almonds, toasted
3   (2-ounce) packages chocolate-covered coffee beans*
      (1 cup)
4   (1.4-ounce) English toffee-flavored candy bars,
      chopped (about 1 cup)

• **Beat** butter and shortening at medium speed of an
electric mixer until creamy; gradually add sugars, beating
well. Add eggs and vanilla; beat well.
• **Combine** flour and next 3 ingredients; add to butter
mixture, beating well. Stir in almonds, coffee beans, and
candy. Cover and chill dough, if desired.
• **Drop** dough by heaping teaspoonfuls onto ungreased
cookie sheets. Bake at 350° for 10 to 11 minutes or until
golden. Cool on cookie sheets 1 minute; remove to wire
racks, and cool completely. **Yield:** 4 dozen.

*Find chocolate-covered coffee beans at a local coffee
house, or see Sources on page 154.

Coffee Bean
Cookies

ALMOND-MINCEMEAT COOKIE CRESCENTS

Mincemeat filling packs these blonde tarts with Christmas flavor.

½ cup butter, softened
¾ cup sugar
1 large egg
1 teaspoon almond extract
2 cups all-purpose flour
1 teaspoon baking powder
½ teaspoon salt
½ cup finely ground blanched almonds
¾ cup mincemeat
¼ cup chopped pecans
1 tablespoon orange juice
1 large egg, lightly beaten
Sugar

• **Beat** butter at medium speed of an electric mixer until creamy; gradually add sugar, beating well. Add 1 egg and almond extract, beating well.
• **Combine** flour and next 3 ingredients; gradually add to butter mixture, beating well. Divide dough into 3 portions; cover and chill 1 hour.
• **Position** knife blade in food processor bowl; add mincemeat, pecans, and orange juice. Process 10 seconds or until finely chopped.
• **Working** with 1 portion of dough at a time, roll out on a floured surface to ⅛" thickness; cut into circles with a 2½" round cutter. Place circles ½" apart on a greased cookie sheet, using a thin spatula.
• **Spoon** about ½ teaspoon mincemeat mixture onto center of each circle. Using spatula, lift and fold each circle in half over filling; press edges together. Press small holes ¼" apart around edges of cookies, using a small wooden skewer. Cut decorative "vents" in cookies, if desired, using a sharp knife. Brush cookies with remaining egg, and sprinkle with sugar. Repeat procedure with remaining dough and mincemeat mixture.
• **Bake** at 350° for 10 to 12 minutes or until golden. Remove to wire racks to cool completely. **Yield:** 4 dozen.

RUM-RAISIN MACAROONS

These easy drop cookies are full of chocolate-covered raisins and coconut.

2 (7-ounce) packages flaked coconut (5⅓ cups)
1 (14-ounce) can sweetened condensed milk
1 cup chopped macadamia nuts, toasted
1 cup chocolate-covered raisins
2 teaspoons vanilla extract
½ teaspoon rum extract

• **Combine** all ingredients in a large bowl; stir well. Drop dough by heaping teaspoonfuls onto parchment paper-lined cookie sheets. Bake at 350° for 10 minutes or until edges are lightly browned. Remove from parchment paper immediately; cool on wire racks. **Yield:** 4 dozen.

VANILLA BEAN CAMEO COOKIES

Once stamped, these vanilla-flecked, chocolate-dipped cookies are almost too pretty to eat. (You don't have to stamp them. They're good plain, too.)

1 cup butter, softened
½ cup sugar
2½ cups all-purpose flour
¼ teaspoon salt
1 whole vanilla bean
1 teaspoon vanilla extract
Christmas cookie stamps (see Sources on page 154)
3 (2-ounce) squares chocolate-flavored or
vanilla-flavored candy coating

• **Beat** butter at medium speed of a heavy-duty electric mixer until creamy; gradually add sugar, beating well.
• **Combine** flour and salt; gradually add to butter mixture, beating until blended after each addition. Split vanilla bean in half lengthwise. Scrape tiny seeds into dough; discard vanilla bean pod. Add vanilla extract to dough. Beat just until blended. Cover and chill dough 1 hour. (Don't chill dough any longer or it will be too firm to roll.)

Vanilla Bean
Cameo Cookies

- **Shape** dough into 1" balls; place balls 2" apart on ungreased cookie sheets. Stamp cookies with cookie stamps.
- **Bake** at 325° for 12 to 13 minutes. Remove cookies to wire racks; cool completely.
- **Melt** candy coating in a small saucepan over low heat, stirring constantly. Transfer to a custard cup, if desired. Dip bottom of cookies in melted candy coating. Turn cookies over on wire rack, so stamp imprint is down. Let stand 1 hour or until chocolate is firm. Yield: 3½ dozen.

Note: Be sure to read the directions that come with your cookie stamp, as they vary from stamp to stamp.

VANILLA BEAN CAMEO COOKIES

Stamp balls of dough with Christmas cookie stamps.

Dip bottoms of cookies in melted candy coating. Turn cookies, dipped side up, on wire racks to dry.

ORANGE-DATE-NUT COOKIES

A great gift to mail—or to keep and serve with hot
orange tea.

1   (10-ounce) package chopped dates
1   teaspoon grated orange rind
1   tablespoon orange juice
1   cup butter or margarine, softened
1½ cups sugar
1   large egg
1   teaspoon vanilla extract
2½ cups all-purpose flour
1½ teaspoons baking powder
½   teaspoon salt
1   cup finely chopped toasted pecans, divided

• **Line** a 9" x 5" x 3" loafpan with aluminum foil, allowing foil to extend over edges of pan. Set aside.
• **Position** knife blade in food processor bowl; add first 3
ingredients. Process 45 seconds or until dates are finely
chopped. Set aside.
• **Beat** butter at medium speed of a heavy-duty electric
mixer until blended. Gradually add sugar, beating until
blended. Add egg and vanilla; beat well. Combine flour,
baking powder, and salt; gradually add to butter mixture,
beating at low speed just until blended.
• **Divide** dough into 3 portions. Knead ½ cup pecans
into 1 portion of dough; press into prepared pan. Knead
date mixture into 1 portion of dough; press in pan over
pecan mixture. Knead remaining ½ cup pecans into
remaining portion of dough; press in pan over date

mixture. Cover and chill at least 2 hours.

• **Invert** loafpan onto a cutting board, removing and discarding aluminum foil. Cut dough lengthwise into 4 sections. Cut each section of dough crosswise into ¼" slices. Place slices 1½" apart on lightly greased cookie sheets.

• **Bake** at 350° for 9 to 10 minutes or until lightly browned. Cool slightly. Remove to wire racks to cool completely. **Yield:** 8 dozen.

ORANGE-DATE-NUT COOKIES

Knead pecans into one third of dough.

Slice each row of chilled dough into ¼" slices.

HERMIT COFFEE BARS

A rich coffee glaze tops these cookie bars spiced with cloves and cinnamon.

1   cup firmly packed brown sugar
½   cup vegetable oil
⅓   cup molasses
¼   cup strongly brewed coffee, cooled
1   teaspoon vanilla extract
2   egg yolks
2½ cups all-purpose flour
1   teaspoon baking soda
1   teaspoon ground cinnamon
½   teaspoon salt
¾   teaspoon ground cloves
½   teaspoon pepper
1   cup raisins
¾   cup chopped pecans
Coffee Glaze

• **Combine** first 6 ingredients, stirring until blended. Combine flour and next 5 ingredients; gradually add to sugar mixture, stirring just until dry ingredients are moistened. Stir in raisins and pecans.

• **Spread** batter in a lightly greased and floured 15" x 10" x 1" jellyroll pan. Bake at 350° for 17 to 18 minutes or until a wooden pick inserted in center comes out clean. Cool in pan; drizzle with Coffee Glaze, using a small spoon. Cut into bars. **Yield:** 4 dozen.

COFFEE GLAZE

2   teaspoons instant coffee granules
1½ tablespoons hot water
1¼ cups sifted powdered sugar

• **Dissolve** coffee granules in hot water, stirring constantly. Add coffee to sugar, and stir until smooth. **Yield:** ½ cup.

Chocolate-Caramel
Thumbprints

CHOCOLATE-CARAMEL THUMBPRINTS

A gooey caramel center guarantees these will disappear quickly from a platter.

½ cup butter or margarine, softened
½ cup sugar
2 (1-ounce) squares semisweet chocolate, melted
1 egg yolk
2 teaspoons vanilla extract
1¼ cups all-purpose flour
¼ teaspoon baking soda
¼ teaspoon salt
¾ cup very finely chopped pecans
16 milk caramels*
2½ tablespoons whipping cream
⅔ cup semisweet chocolate morsels
2 teaspoons shortening

• **Beat** butter at medium speed of an electric mixer until creamy; gradually add sugar, beating well. Add melted chocolate and egg yolk, beating until blended. Stir in vanilla.

• **Combine** flour, soda, and salt; add to butter mixture, beating well. Cover and chill 1 hour.

• **Shape** dough into 1" balls; roll balls in chopped pecans. Place balls 1" apart on greased cookie sheets. Press thumb gently into center of each ball, leaving an indentation.

• **Bake** at 350° for 12 minutes or until set. Meanwhile, combine caramels and whipping cream in top of a double boiler over simmering water. Cook over medium-low heat, stirring constantly, until caramels melt and mixture is smooth.

• **Remove** cookies from oven; cool slightly, and press center of each cookie again. Quickly spoon ¾ teaspoon caramel mixture into center of each cookie. Remove cookies to wire racks to cool.

• **Place** chocolate morsels and shortening in a heavy-duty, zip-top plastic bag; seal bag. Microwave at HIGH 1 to 1½ minutes; squeeze bag until chocolate melts. Snip a tiny hole in one corner of bag, using scissors. Drizzle chocolate over cooled cookies. **Yield:** about 2½ dozen.

*For milk caramels, we used Brach's.

Mixed Nut
Turtles

MIXED NUT TURTLES

A patty of melted chocolate nestles between salty nuts on this candylike cookie.

¾ cup butter, softened

½ cup sugar

1 egg yolk

1 teaspoon vanilla extract

1½ cups all-purpose flour

1 (9.75-ounce) can mixed nuts (with almonds, macadamia nuts, and cashews)

1½ cups semisweet chocolate morsels

2 teaspoons shortening

• **Beat** butter at medium speed of an electric mixer until creamy; gradually add sugar, beating well. Add yolk and vanilla, beating well. Add flour, beating just until blended.

• **Drop** dough by level tablespoonfuls 2" apart onto ungreased cookie sheets. Flatten each ball of dough to a 2" circle, using fingers. Cut large macadamia nuts in half. Press nuts firmly into outside top edges of cookies.

• **Bake** at 350° for 10 to 12 minutes or until edges of cookies are lightly browned. Cool on cookie sheets 1 minute. Carefully remove cookies to wire racks to cool completely.

• **Place** chocolate and shortening in top of a double boiler over hot water; stir until melted. Spoon 1 heaping teaspoon melted chocolate onto center of each cookie. Spread and smooth chocolate between nuts. Let set until chocolate hardens. **Yield:** 26 cookies.

MIXED NUT TURTLES

Press nuts firmly into outside top edges of cookies.

Peppermint Candy Shortbread

PEPPERMINT CANDY SHORTBREAD

Sprinkle crushed peppermint candy on these vanilla-dipped shortbread triangles.

1 cup butter, softened
⅓ cup sugar
2½ cups all-purpose flour
8 ounces vanilla-flavored candy coating
⅔ cup crushed hard peppermint candy

• **Beat** butter at medium speed of an electric mixer until creamy; gradually add sugar, beating well. Add flour, beating just until blended.
• **Divide** dough into 3 equal portions. Place 1 portion of dough on an ungreased cookie sheet; roll into a 6" circle. Score dough into 8 triangles. Repeat procedure with remaining 2 portions of dough.
• **Bake** at 325° for 25 minutes or until barely golden. Cool on cookie sheets 5 minutes. Remove from cookie sheets, and cool completely on wire racks. Working very carefully, separate disks into wedges. (Shortbread is a fragile cookie. Be gentle with it so tips remain intact.)
• **Melt** candy coating in top of a double boiler over hot water. Remove from heat. Carefully dip wide edges of shortbread in melted coating; place shortbread on wax paper. Sprinkle crushed candy over coated edges. Let stand until coating is hardened. **Yield:** 2 dozen.

Note: See Sources on page 154 for ordering information on specialty peppermint candies.

Slice shortbread disks into wedges.

Carefully dip wide edges of shortbread into candy coating.

WHITE-ON-WHITE ORNAMENTS

Press modeling clay into cookie molds and embellish with beads.
Make several to give teachers and co-workers.

For 1 ornament:

large cookie mold

air-drying modeling compound (We used Crayola Model
   Magic. A 12-ounce package makes 3 ornaments.)

assorted plastic pearl beads

clear acrylic spray sealer

1 yard 1⅝"-wide ribbon

1. To mold the ornament, wash and dry the cookie mold.
Press the modeling compound into the mold with your
fingers. Cover the mold with a sheet of paper, and use a
rolling pin to push the compound firmly into the mold.
Remove the paper. Using a table knife, gently remove the
shape from the mold. Place the ornament, flat side down,
on top of the paper. Use a drinking straw to punch a hole
in the ornament for the ribbon hanger.

2. To embellish the ornament, place pearl beads on the
ornament as desired. (To make it easier, before placing
the beads, make small indentations in the ornament with
a wooden skewer or toothpick.) Gently press the beads
into the ornament. Following manufacturer's directions,
let the ornament dry. Spray the ornament with acrylic
sealer. Let dry. Thread the ribbon through the hole in the
ornament and tie the ends in a bow.

Note: For cookie molds, see Sources on page 154.

PEARL TASSEL

This tassel makes a pretty decorative accent atop packages or on the tree.

To make the tassel, you will need a wooden candle cup and 2 to 4 packages of plastic pearls-by-the-yard. (Each package has approximately 4 yards of pearls. Both items are available at craft stores.)

Paint the candle cup white. Let dry. To form a hanger, fold a 5" length of narrow cording or ribbon in half, and hot-glue the ends to the center bottom of the candle cup. (The bottom of the candle cup will become the top of the tassel.) Wrap the candle cup with the pearls, hot-gluing at regular intervals to hold the pearls in place and covering the ribbon ends with pearls. (For the tassel pictured, we left the rim of the candle cup uncovered.)

For the tassel, loop strands of pearls to the length and thickness desired. Using thin craft wire or thread, tie the pearl strands together at the center top, and clip the loops apart at the center bottom. Hot-glue the top of the tassel into the candle cup.

Bead-Top
Tassel

DECORATOR TASSELS

These gifts make pretty accents for chairs and doorknobs year-round.

For Each Tassel:
diagrams on page 147
craft glue
approximately 110 yards yarn
11" cardboard square
12" length of wire
craft knife
yarn needle

For the Bead-Top Tassel:
2"-diameter unfinished wooden bead (or 2"-diameter
    unfinished wooden drawer pull with hole drilled
    through center)
2 (20-mm to 25-mm) beads (We painted 1 unfinished
    wooden 20-mm bead and used 1 [25-mm] plastic
    bead.)
unfinished wooden disk with a center hole (available at
    craft stores)
acrylic paint in desired colors
clear acrylic spray
3 gold-colored beads in desired shapes and sizes

For the Bell-Top Tassel:
unfinished wooden bell-shaped doll body (available in
    doll-making section of craft stores)
assorted wooden beads
8" (⅜"-diameter) decorative cording

1. To make the bead-top tassel, paint the wooden beads and the wooden disk in the desired colors and patterns. Let dry. Spray all the pieces with clear acrylic. Let dry. Glue the wooden disk to the bottom of the largest bead to add stability to the beaded top.

To make the bell-top tassel, working on half of the bell at a time, cover the bell with a thin layer of glue, and wrap it tightly with yarn.

2. To make the cord, cut 3 (40") lengths of yarn. Tie all 3 lengths together at 1 end and twist them until tight. Knot the other end, and then tie the 2 knotted ends together, leaving approximately 4" loose below the knot to tie around the tassel.

3. To make the tassel, wrap the yarn around an 11" cardboard square 140 times. Insert a 12" length of wire under the strands along the top edge of the cardboard. Loosely pull the wire together, twisting it once to hold the yarn in place. Using a craft knife, cut the yarn along the bottom edge of the cardboard. Pull the wire tightly around the yarn, twisting it to secure. Trim the excess wire.

4. To assemble the tassel, thread the looped end of the cord onto a yarn needle, and pull the cord up through the beads and/or bell. For the bead-top tassel, begin with the wooden disk and 2" bead, and follow with a gold-colored bead, a 25-mm bead, a gold-colored bead, a 20-mm bead, and a gold-colored bead. For the bell-top tassel, begin with the bell and follow with assorted wooden beads in the desired order. Before securing the top bead with a knot, tie the 4" loose ends of cord tightly around the wire and tassel. Then pull the tassel tightly against the beads, and tie a knot above the top bead. Trim the tassel bottom with sharp scissors. (See the diagrams on page 147.)

For the bell-top tassel, glue decorative cording around the bottom of the bell.

Bell-Top Tassel

HOLIDAY OIL LAMP

Use a variety of bottle shapes and sizes—even colors—to make one-of-a-kind gifts.

glass bottle

glass marbles or beads

candlewick

large heat-resistant bead with center hole to fit bottle top
 (Use glass, stone, or metal beads. Do not use beads
 made of plastic or ceramic.)

funnel

candle or lamp oil (Pure paraffin oil is recommended for
 its odorless and smokeless qualities.)

1. To make the oil lamp, wash the glass bottle and let it dry completely. Fill the bottle to the desired level with glass marbles or beads.

2. To make the wick, cut a piece of candlewick the length of the bottle. Thread the wick through the center of the large bead. Using a funnel, fill the bottle with lamp oil. Place the bead with the wick on top of the bottle. Gently move the bottle so the wick is centered among the marbles.

Trim the wick to approximately ⅛" above the bead. (A shorter wick prevents excess smoke.) Allow at least 5 minutes for the wick to absorb the oil before lighting.

Note: For gift giving, you may want to remove the wick and cork the bottle. You can also give the bottle unfilled, and include a separate bottle of lamp oil.

LAMP VARIATIONS

• Lamp oil can be scented with just a few drops of essential oil.

• Instead of a bead, use a brass or steel washer from the hardware store to hold the wick.

• 100%-cotton shoelaces can be used for the candlewick.

• Use natural stones, shells, charms, or dried flowers and spices to fill the bottle.

Noel Pillow

CROSS-STITCH PILLOWS

Start early on the cross-stitching for these decorative, handmade pillows.

For Each Pillow:

graphs and diagram on pages 152–153

12"-wide x 8"-high rectangle 30-count linen cross-stitch fabric

embroidery floss

¼ yard fusible interfacing

⅓ yard velvet

1 yard ¼"-diameter polyester cable cording

polyester stuffing

For the Noel Pillow:

Following the graph, cross-stitch the pattern, working over 2 threads and centering the design on the linen piece.

For the Monogram Pillow:

Following the graph, cross-stitch the middle initial, working over 2 threads and centering the letter on the linen piece. Place the first and last initial 3 or 4 spaces from the center letter.

For Both Pillows:

1. To make the pillow, when the cross-stitching is complete, wash and iron the linen. Following manufacturer's directions, apply the fusible interfacing to the wrong side of the linen.

Trim the linen to a 9½"-wide x 6"-high rectangle, centering the design. Cut a 9½"-wide x 6"-high rectangle of velvet. Cut a 1½" x 30" bias strip of velvet for the piping.

2. To trim the pillow, with wrong sides facing, wrap the bias strip of velvet around the cable cording. Using a zipper or cording foot, machine-baste the piping to the linen piece, keeping the raw edges even. Start and finish by turning in the bias ends at the center of the bottom edge. (See the diagram on page 152.)

3. To complete the pillow, with right sides facing, stitch the velvet to the linen, stitching on top of the basting stitches and leaving a 4" opening for turning. Trim the seam and turn the pillow right side out. Fill the pillow with polyester stuffing. Slipstitch the opening closed.

Monogram Pillow

CHRISTMAS CARDIGAN

Make over a simple sweatshirt with a little cut-and-sew
magic and some pretty crocheted doilies.

diagrams on page 151
navy blue sweatshirt
chalk pencil
7 snowflake-look crocheted doilies
invisible thread
4 yards silver cording
tapestry needle

1. To prepare the sweatshirt, cut the ribbing from the bottom. Lay the sweatshirt flat on a cutting surface. Align the shoulders and sides and trim the bottom edge even.

To turn the sweatshirt into a cardigan, using a ruler and chalk pencil, draw a line down the center front of the sweatshirt. Cut along this line. Zigzag or serge the center front and bottom edges.

2. To finish the edges, with right sides facing, turn up a 2" hem along the bottom, and stitch the hem to the center front 1" from the edge. Trim the corners at the bottom front edges, then turn them right side out. Turn under 1" on the center front edges. Stitch 1" from the center front and 2" from the bottom edges (see diagrams).

3. To add the snowflakes, referring to the photograph, position the doilies on the cardigan front and back. Using invisible thread, stitch along the outer edges of the doilies.

4. To add the cording, thread the cording through the eye of a tapestry needle. Take a stitch through the cardigan just under the edge of the doily. Remove the needle and knot the cording on the inside of the cardigan. On the outside, wind and loop the cording to another doily (refer to the photograph for positioning). Hold the cording in place with straight pins. Cut the cording, leaving a 3" tail. Stitch the tail under the edge of the doily, knotting the cording on the inside as before. Using invisible thread, whipstitch the cording in place. Remove the pins. Continue for the remaining doilies.

PATTERNS
GARDEN ACCENTS ORNAMENTS
Instructions begin on page 19.
Patterns are full-size.

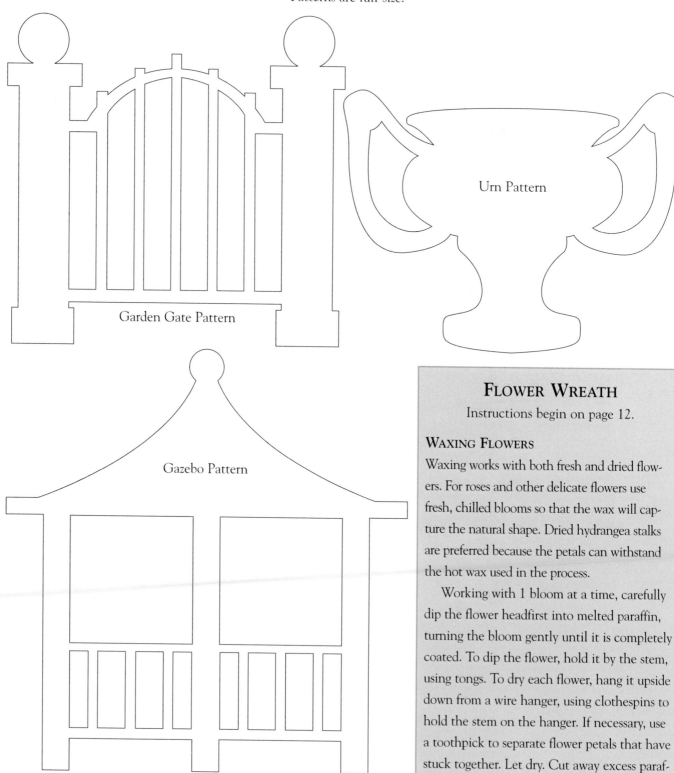

Garden Gate Pattern

Urn Pattern

Gazebo Pattern

FLOWER WREATH
Instructions begin on page 12.

WAXING FLOWERS
Waxing works with both fresh and dried flowers. For roses and other delicate flowers use fresh, chilled blooms so that the wax will capture the natural shape. Dried hydrangea stalks are preferred because the petals can withstand the hot wax used in the process.

Working with 1 bloom at a time, carefully dip the flower headfirst into melted paraffin, turning the bloom gently until it is completely coated. To dip the flower, hold it by the stem, using tongs. To dry each flower, hang it upside down from a wire hanger, using clothespins to hold the stem on the hanger. If necessary, use a toothpick to separate flower petals that have stuck together. Let dry. Cut away excess paraffin around the edges of the flower.

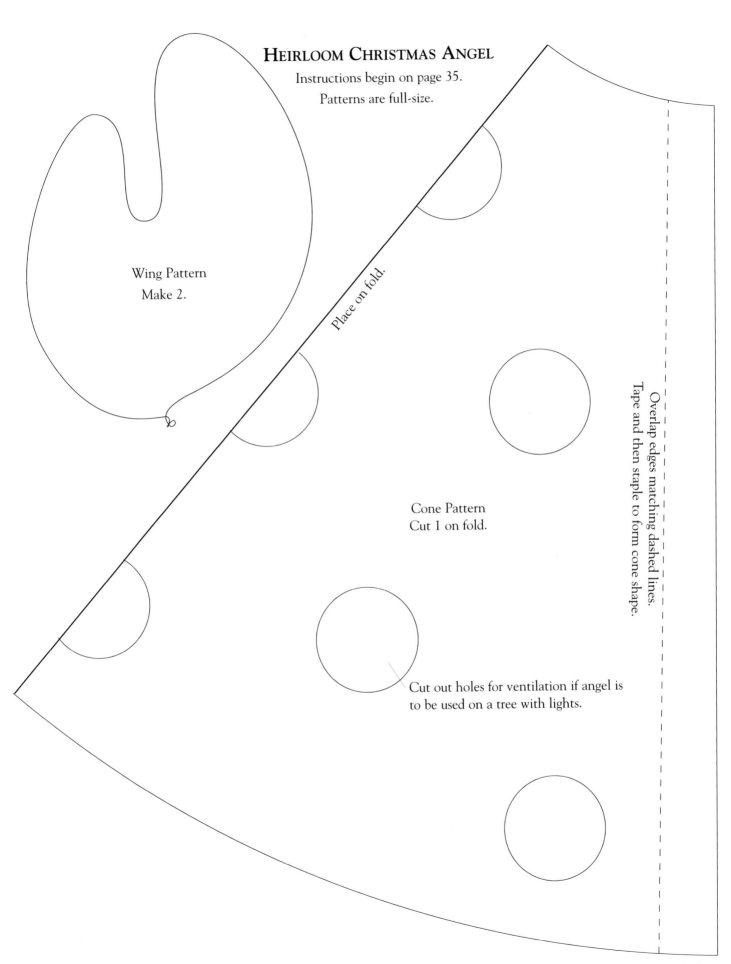

HEIRLOOM CHRISTMAS ANGEL
Instructions begin on page 35.
Patterns are full-size.

Wing Pattern
Make 2.

Place on fold.

Cone Pattern
Cut 1 on fold.

Cut out holes for ventilation if angel is
to be used on a tree with lights.

Overlap edges matching dashed lines.
Tape and then staple to form cone shape.

HEIRLOOM CHRISTMAS ANGEL

Instructions begin on page 35.
Pattern is full-size.

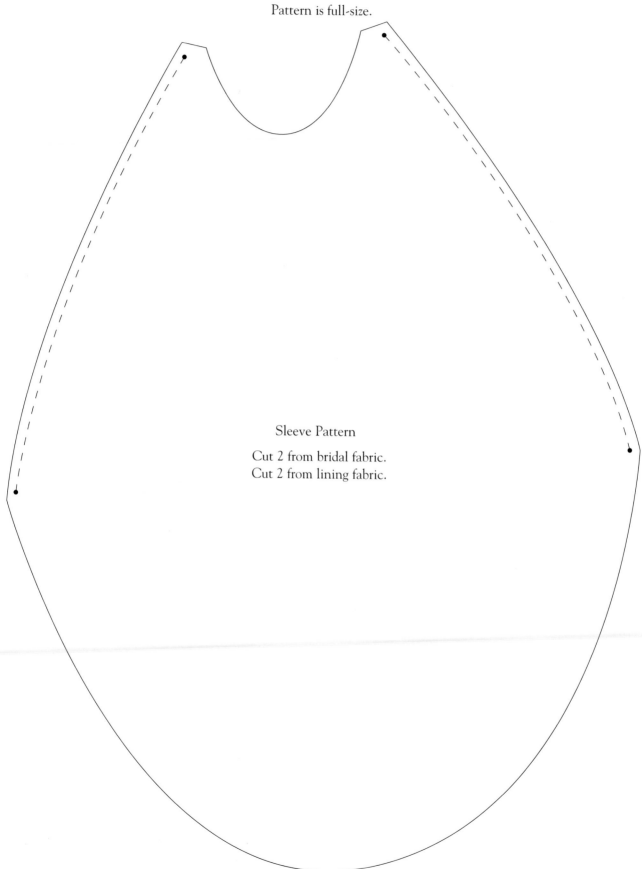

Sleeve Pattern

Cut 2 from bridal fabric.
Cut 2 from lining fabric.

HEIRLOOM CHRISTMAS ANGEL

Instructions begin on page 35.

Pattern is full-size.

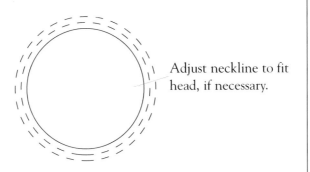

Bodice Pattern
Cut 1 from bridal fabric.

Adjust neckline to fit head, if necessary.

Instructions begin on page 35.

MAKING A BOW

For an 8"-wide bow, you will need 4 yards of wire-edged ribbon. To make the bow, measure 4" from the end of the ribbon. Pinch the ribbon between your forefinger and thumb. (This is the center point of the bow.) Make a 4" loop and pinch the ribbon again at the center (Diagram 1).

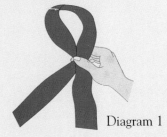

Diagram 1

Twist the ribbon one-half turn and make a loop on the opposite side. Make 5 loops on either side of the center in the same manner (Diagram 2). Fold a 9" length of florist's wire over the center of the bow.

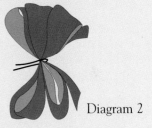

Diagram 2

Fold the bow in half across the wire. Holding the bow firmly, twist the wire ends together (Diagram 3). Fluff the bow by pulling firmly on the loops. To add streamers to the bow, cut ribbon in the desired lengths and secure it with wire at the back of the bow.

Diagram 3

MONOGRAMMED STOCKING

Instructions begin on page 31.

Pattern is full-size.

Monogrammed Stocking Pattern

Extend lines for pattern, as directed in Step 1.

146

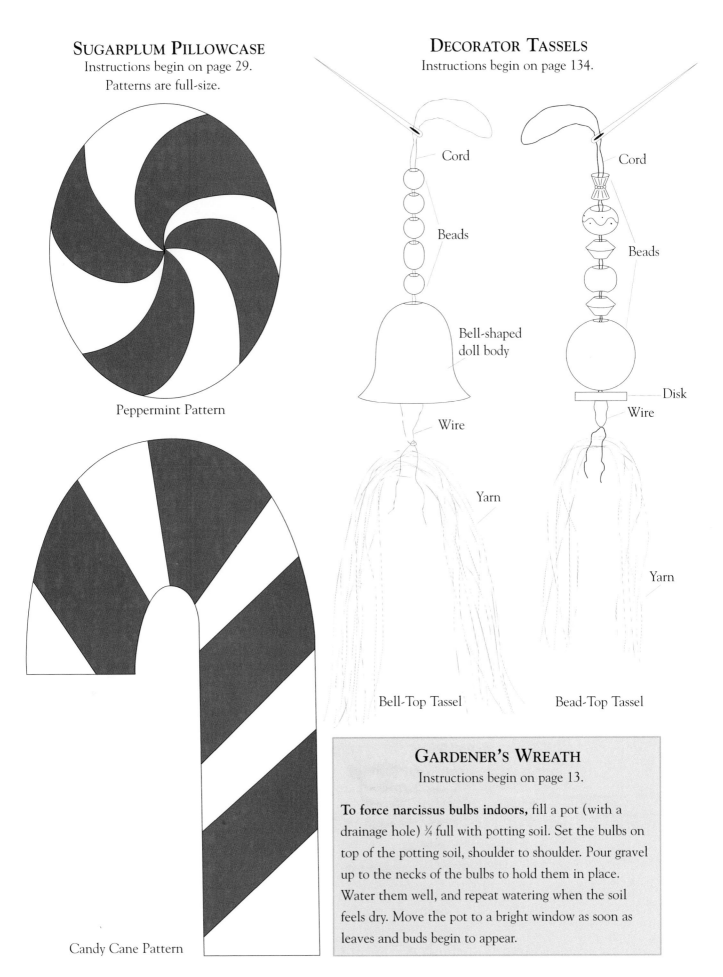

SUGARPLUM PILLOWCASE
Instructions begin on page 29.
Patterns are full-size.

Peppermint Pattern

Candy Cane Pattern

DECORATOR TASSELS
Instructions begin on page 134.

Cord

Beads

Bell-shaped
doll body

Wire

Yarn

Bell-Top Tassel

Cord

Beads

Disk

Wire

Yarn

Bead-Top Tassel

GARDENER'S WREATH
Instructions begin on page 13.

To force narcissus bulbs indoors, fill a pot (with a drainage hole) ¾ full with potting soil. Set the bulbs on top of the potting soil, shoulder to shoulder. Pour gravel up to the necks of the bulbs to hold them in place. Water them well, and repeat watering when the soil feels dry. Move the pot to a bright window as soon as leaves and buds begin to appear.

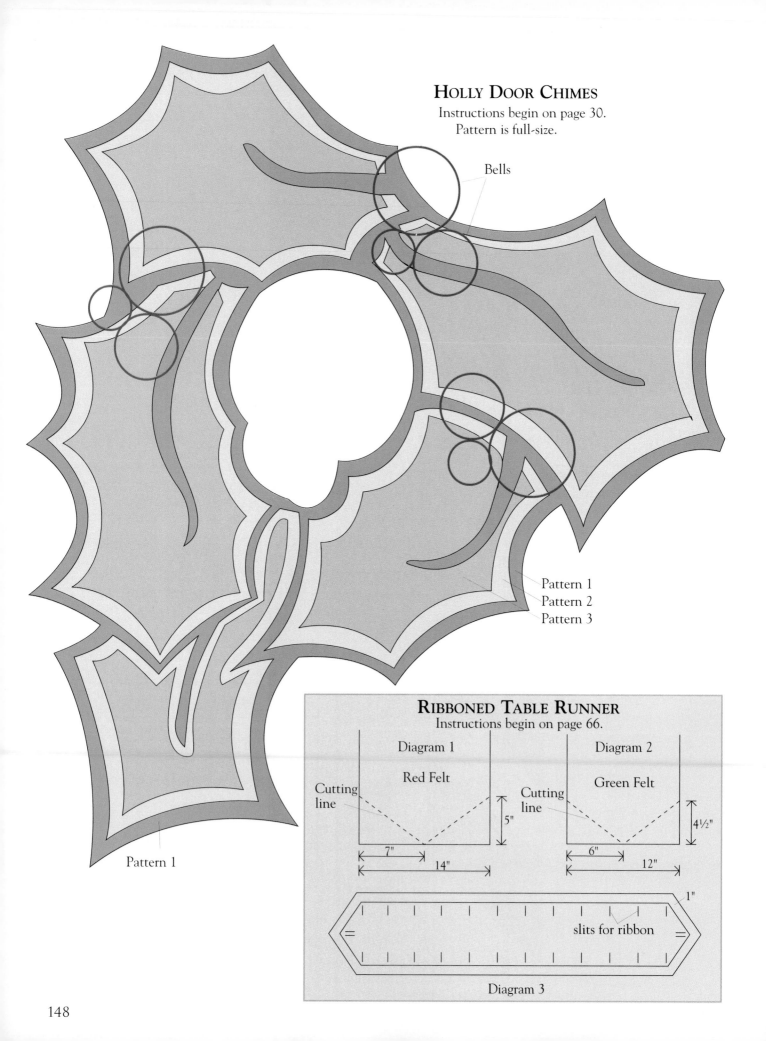

HOLLY DOOR CHIMES
Instructions begin on page 30.
Pattern is full-size.

Bells

Pattern 1
Pattern 2
Pattern 3

Pattern 1

RIBBONED TABLE RUNNER
Instructions begin on page 66.

Diagram 1

Red Felt

Cutting
line

5"

7"

14"

Diagram 2

Green Felt

Cutting
line

4½"

6"

12"

1"

slits for ribbon

Diagram 3

VELVET STOCKINGS
Instructions begin on page 32.

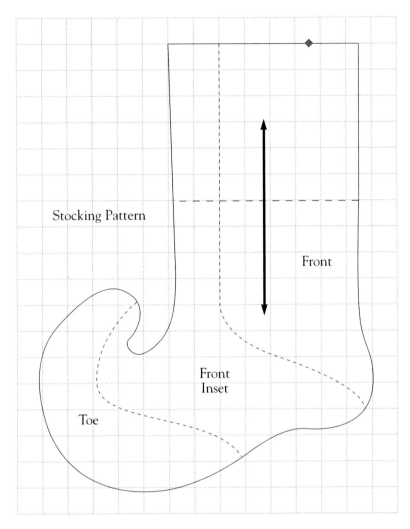

Stocking Pattern

Front

Toe

Front
Inset

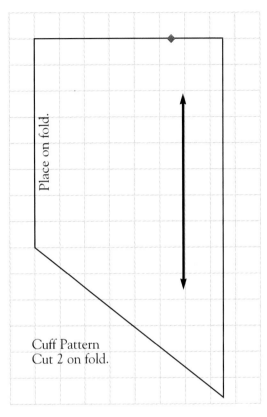

Place on fold.

Cuff Pattern
Cut 2 on fold.

Each square = 1".
Pattern includes ⅝" seam allowances.

For Velvet & Brocade Stocking:
   Front - Cut 1 from brocade.
   Toe - Cut 1 from brocade.
   Front Inset - Cut 1 from velvet.
   Stocking Back - Cut 1 from velvet.

For Velvet & Fringe Stocking:
   Stocking - Cut 2 from velvet.

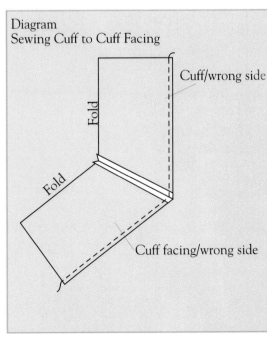

Diagram
Sewing Cuff to Cuff Facing

Cuff/wrong side

Fold

Fold

Cuff facing/wrong side

MAILING BOWS

Instructions begin on page 113.

Patterns are full-size.

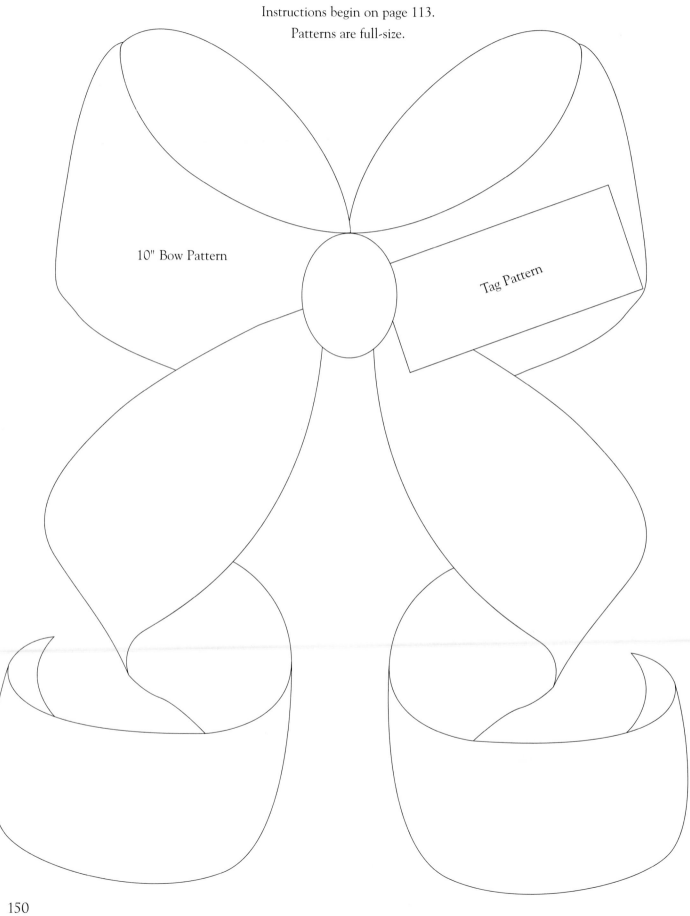

10" Bow Pattern

Tag Pattern

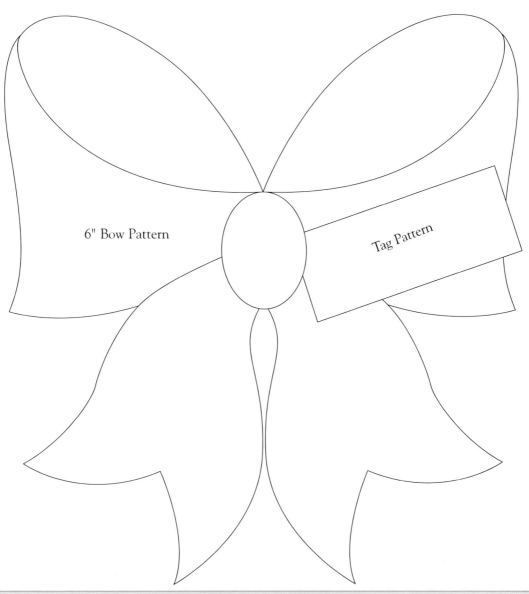

6" Bow Pattern

Tag Pattern

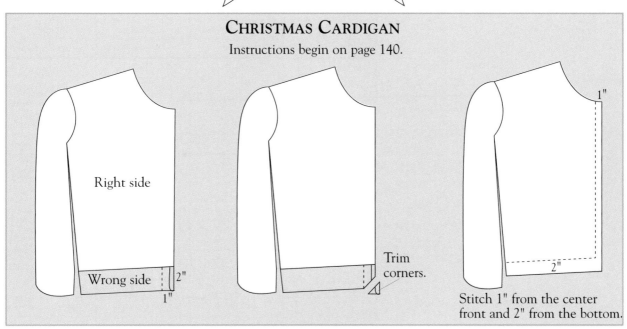

CHRISTMAS CARDIGAN
Instructions begin on page 140.

Right side

Wrong side   2"
1"

Trim corners.

1"

2"

Stitch 1" from the center front and 2" from the bottom.

CROSS-STITCH PILLOWS

Instructions begin on page 139.

Floss List:

Symbol	Type	Number	Color
●	DMC	701	Christmas Green-LT
＊	DMC	321	Christmas Red

Diagram

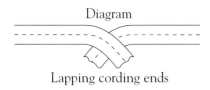

Lapping cording ends

TABLECLOTH TREE SKIRT

Instructions begin on page 26.

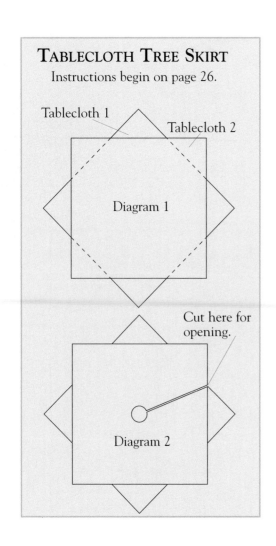

Tablecloth 1

Tablecloth 2

Diagram 1

Cut here for opening.

Diagram 2

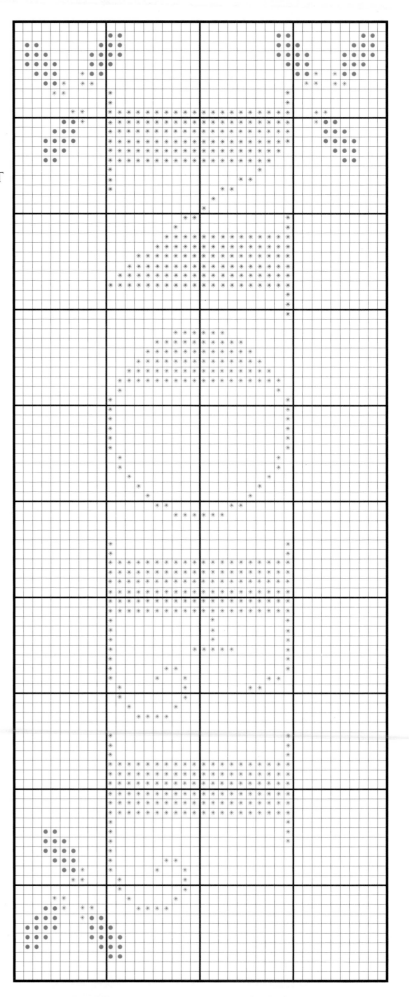

SOURCES

Source information current at time of publication

Red Berry Wreath, page 10

Pages 10–11—holly: Green Valley Growers, 10450 Cherry Ridge Rd., Sebastopol, CA 95472, or call (707) 823-5583.
straw wreath: Schrock's Int'l, 110 Water St., P.O. Box 538, Bolivar, OH 44612, or call (330) 874-3700.

Page 11—plastic water vials: Contact Kervar, www.Kervar.com, or call (212) 564-2525.

Page 12—freeze-dried flowers: Meadow Everlastings, 16464 Shabbona Rd., Malta, IL 60150, or call (815) 825-2539.
straw wreath: Schrock's Int'l, 110 Water St., P.O. Box 538, Bolivar, OH 44612, or call (330) 874-3700.

Pages 14–19—gardener's tree accessories: Wildflower Designs, 2807 Second Ave. S., Birmingham, AL 35223, or call (205) 322-1311.
garden fencing: For information on stores carrying Walnut Hollow Woodcraft products, call (608) 935-2341.

Styrofoam ball: Schrock's Int'l, 110 Water St., P.O. Box 538, Bolivar, OH 44612, or call (330) 874-3700.

Page 21—ornaments: Pier 1 Imports, Hoover, AL (205) 733-8016.

Page 22—velvet: For information on stores carrying Waverly velvet, call (800) 423-5881.

Page 24—Styrofoam forms: Schrock's Int'l, 110 Water St., P.O. Box 538, Bolivar, OH 44612, or call (330) 874-3700.
dried herbs: Tom Thumb Workshops, 14100 Lankford Hwy./ P.O. Box 357, Mappsville, VA 23407. Call (757) 824-3507 for a free catalog.

Page 29—pillowcase: Contact Eddie Bauer, www.eddiebauer.com, or call (800) 426-8020.

Page 30—felt: Contact Kunin Felt at kuninfelt.com, or call (603) 929-6100 for mail-order prices.

Pages 32–33—fabric and trims: M's Fabric Gallery, 200 21st Street S., Birmingham, AL 35233, or call (800) 467-3065.
candy: Hammond's Candies Since 1920, 2550 W 29th Ave., Denver, CO 80211, or call (888) CANDY-99.

Pages 34–41—decorative trims and cordings: Heritage Trimming, 32 Library Street, Suncook, NH 03275, or call (603) 485-7800.
ribbons: C. M. Offray & Son, Inc., Rt. 24 - Box 601, Chester, NJ 07930-0601.

fabric, lace, and gold-white braid: Sewsational Fine Fabrics, 5975 Roswell Road, Atlanta, GA 30328.
doll head and arms: Opal Doll Fashions, 1672 Lilburn–Stone Mtn. Rd., Stone Mountain, GA 30087.
star charm: Creative Beginnings, P.O. Box 1330, Morro Bay, CA 93443, or call (800) 367-1739.
doll making materials: Schrock's Int'l, 110 Water St., P.O. Box 538, Bolivar, OH 44612, or call (330) 874-3700.
doll making supplies: Kirchen Bros., Box 1016, Skokie, IL 60076, or call (708) 647-6747 for free catalog.
doll making tools: Pierce Tools, 1610 Parkdale Dr., Grants Pass, OR 97527, or call (503) 476-1778.

Pages 42–43—green pots: Potluck Studios, 23 Main St., Accord, NY 12404, or call (914) 626-2300.

Page 45—casserole dish: Sadek, 125 Beechwood Ave., New York, NY 10802, or call (914) 633-8090.

Page 48—plate: The Loom Co., 246 E. 48th St., New York, NY 10017, or call (212) 366-7214.

Page 64—gold-rimmed chargers: Table Matters, Birmingham, AL (205) 879-0125.

Page 65—wooden plate: For information on stores carrying Walnut Hollow Woodcraft products, call (608) 935-2341.

Page 66—felt: Contact Kunin Felt at kuninfelt.com, or call (603) 929-6100 for mail-order prices.

Page 69—punch bowl: Daisy Arts, P.O. Box 2255, Venice, CA 90294, or call (310) 396-8463.
glasses: Union Street Glass, 833 S. 19th St., Richmond, CA 94804, or call (888) 451-7752.

Page 75—Styrofoam cone: Schrock's Int'l, 110 Water St., P.O. Box 538, Bolivar, OH 44612, or call (330) 874-3700.
clothesline wire: Dand-o-line, Anchorwire, 425 Church St., Goodlettsville, TN 37072.

Page 83—fondue pot: Contact Williams-Sonoma at (800) 541-1262.

Page 86—candle holder: Lamb's Ears, Ltd, Birmingham, AL (205) 969-3138.
pedestal: Dover Metals, 4768 Hwy M63, Coloma, MI 49038, or call (616) 849-1411.
ribbon: Vaban Gille, Inc., P.O. Box 420747, San Francisco, CA 94142, or call (417) 552-5490.

Orange Pomanders, page 86

Page 87—Styrofoam cone: Schrock's Int'l, 110 Water St., P.O. Box 538, Bolivar, OH 44612, or call (330) 874-3700.
glass containers: Contact Crate & Barrel at (800) 451-8217.
candles: Contact Illuminations at (800) 226-3537.

Page 96—tray: Sadek, 125 Beechwood Ave., New York, NY 10802, or call (914) 633-8090.

Page 98—cup and saucer: Contact Williams-Sonoma at (800) 541-1262.

Pages 102–103—tray: Stonefish Pottery, 127 Girard Ave., Hartford, CT 06105, or call (203) 547-0800.

Page 109—dishes: Contact Williams-Sonoma at (800) 541-1262.

Page 110—burlap, twine, kraft paper: Contact Loose Ends at www.loosend.com, or call (503) 390-7457.
ribbon: Mokuba Ribbons, 561 7th Ave. 11th Flr., New York, NY 10018, or call (212) 221-6663.

Page 113—gift wrap: For information on stores carrying Caspari gift wrap, call (800) CASPARI.

Page 114—chocolate-covered coffee beans: Barnie's Coffee & Tea Company, (800) 284-1416.

Page 116—cookie stamp: To find a Michael's Arts and Craft Store nearest you, call (800) 642-4235.

Page 117—tray: Christine's, 2417 Montevallo Road, Birmingham, AL 35223, or call (205) 871-8297.

Page 123—pedestal: Sadek, 125 Beechwood Ave., New York, NY 10802, or call (914) 633-8090.

Page 129—hard peppermints: Hammond's Candies Since 1920, 2550 W 29th Ave., Denver, CO 80211, or call (888) CANDY-99.

Page 130—plate: Bromberg's, 2800 Cahaba Rd., Birmingham, AL 35352, or call (205) 871-3276.

Page 132—cookie mold: Cookie Art Exchange, P.O. Box 4267, Manchester, NH 03108-42677, or call (603) 668-5900.
modeling compound: Look for Crayola® Model Magic at art and craft stores.

Page 133—pearls: Schrock's Int'l, 110 Water St., P.O. Box 538, Bolivar, OH 44612, or call (330) 874-3700.

Page 134—wooden beads: Schrock's Int'l, 110 Water St., P.O. Box 538, Bolivar, OH 44612, or call (330) 874-3700.
yarn: Memory Hagler Knitting Etc., Vestavia Hills, AL (205) 822-7875.

Page 136—glass beads: Pier 1 Imports, Hoover, AL (205) 733-8016.

Page 141—sweatshirt: Contact L. L. Bean, Inc., www.llbean.com, or call (800) 341-4341.

General Index

The Gift of Velvet,
page 22

Tablecloth Tree Skirt,
page 26

RECIPE INDEX

CONTRIBUTORS

Velvet & Fringe
Stocking, page 32

DESIGNERS

Peggy Barnhart, red berry wreath, 10

Cathy Blach, flower wreath, 12; chair swag and tree topper, 67

Elizabeth Carnegie-Taylor, angel, 34–41; photographs, 36–40

Janice Cox, oil lamps, 136

Jan Gautro, centerpieces, 87

Charlotte Hagood, topiaries, 24

Linda Hendrickson, pillowcase, 29; door chimes, 30; stocking, 32

Margot Hotchkiss, stocking, 31; wooden plate, 65; orange pomanders, 86; gift wraps, 110–111; tassel, 133

Duffy Morrison, napkin mantel scarf, 21; velvet pillows, 22; stocking, 33; pillows, 138–139

Dondra G. Parham, tree skirt, 26; napkin ties, 65; napkin trees, 75; frames, 112; ornaments, 132

Katie Stoddard, tassels, 134–135

Carole Sullivan, pomegranate wreath, 11; tomato cage trees, 72–73

Sybil Sylvester, gardener's wreath, 13; gardener's tree, 14–19; apple chandelier, 20

Kelley Taylor, ornaments, 27

Cynthia Moody Wheeler, table runner, 66; mailing bows, 113; cardigan, 140

Peggy Ann Williams, coffee votives, 74

RECIPE DEVELOPERS

Alison Lewis

Elizabeth Tyler Luckett

Debby Maugans Nakos

Oxmoor House Test Kitchens Staff

Thanks to the following homeowners:

Pam and Tom Buck

Alice Cox

Catherine and Ted Pewitt

Carole and David Sullivan

Leslie and John Simpson

Sally and Jeff Threlkeld

Kay Till

Dolly and James Walker

Madeline and Bill White

Kay and Tom Worley